Liesl Ujvary
Good & Safe

translated from German by
Ann Cotten & Anna-Isabella Dinwoodie

introduction by Fatima Naqvi

 WORLD POETRY

Good & Safe
Copyright © Liesl Ujvary, 1977
Copyright © Liesl Ujvary & Klever Verlag, 2017, 2025
English translation copyright © Ann Cotten & Anna-Isabella Dinwoodie, 2025
Translators' Notes © Ann Cotten & Anna-Isabella Dinwoodie, 2025

Originally published as *Sicher & Gut* in 1977 by Rhombus Verlag in Vienna, Austria, and republished by Klever Verlag, Vienna, in 2017.

First Edition, First Printing, 2025
ISBN 978-1-954218-37-6

World Poetry Books
New York, NY
worldpoetrybooks.com

World Poetry titles are distributed by Asterism Books (US) and Turnaround Publisher Services (UK). Subscriptions and standing orders are available.

Library of Congress Control Number: 2025943370

Cover design by Andrew Bourne
Typesetting by Don't Look Now
Printed in Lithuania by BALTO Print

The translation of this book was supported by the Deutscher Übersetzerfonds (German Translators' Fund).

World Poetry Books is a 501(c)(3) nonprofit and charitable organization founded in 2017 in New York City and a member of the Community of Literary Magazines and Presses (CLMP).

World Poetry's publications and programs are made possible by grants from the Poetry Foundation, Hawthornden Foundation, and the New York State Council on the Arts with the support of the Office of the Governor and the New York State Legislature, and supported by an affiliation with the Humanities Institute and the Translation Program at the University of Connecticut (Storrs), as well as individual donors and our subscribers. To learn more about supporting World Poetry, please visit our website: worldpoetrybooks.com/support.

Contents

vii   Introduction by Fatima Naqvi

      Good & Safe
17   What Holds the World Together
61   Do You Not Sense Anything?
95   Poems About Poems
111   Novels About Novels
123   I
143   Autobiography with Instructions

167   Notes from the Translators
175   thanks

Read This Book: It Makes You Feel *Good & Safe*

AT THE TIME I read Liesl Ujvary's *Good & Safe*, I was thinking a lot about AI and its implications for my line of work as a professor of literature. It seemed that her book, with its lists, instructions, and programs for a good life, however defined, was commenting on the very situation in which I found myself.

The more I played around with artificial intelligence, with ChatGPT and its accomplices, the more frightened I became. The clearly written prose text is dead. Even the unclear prose text is dead. The machine revises the Germanic phrases that sneak into my English, irons out its kinks, rearranges excessive subordinate clauses, and unentangles my formerly dangling prepositions, which I overcorrect—sounding stodgy and needlessly professorial. It offers succinct, if occasionally wrong, introductions to anything you feed into it. Like my students after an all-nighter, it sometimes "hallucinates" (the technical term for its errors).

WHAT CAN STILL escape the machine? Can poetry evade its maw? After all, every word in a poem is asked to do so much—to create ambivalence, rhythm, surprise, sonority. Yet even in the case of poetry, AI is able to mimic the mellifluous, the metrically sophisticated, and the extraordinarily ordinary. And it will get better at doing so. In preparing this introduction to Liesl Ujvary's *Good & Safe*, I entered the prompt "post-war concrete poetry," the global experimental movement of the 1950s through the early 1970s to which she peripherally belongs. To compare Ujvary's playful texts from the 1970s with ChatGPT's output, I asked it for a concrete poem in German. The query gave me this:

>
knospe
>hoffnung
>wächst, still
>im schattenlicht
>des alten erinnerns

> wurzeln graben geschichten
> in erde, feucht vom vergangenen
> leben. blätter flüstern vom morgen
> der noch nicht war. ein baum, ein atem,
> ein wort. und wieder beginnt der kreis.

ChatGPT then offered the following translation into English:

> bud
> hope
> grows, quietly
> in shadowed light
> of old remembering
> roots dig up old stories
> in soil, damp with the past
> life. leaves whisper of the day
> not yet born. a tree, a breath,
> a word. and the circle begins again.

Let's leave aside whether this example tilts into corniness, and let's bracket the focus on nature, which is out of keeping with the German concrete poetry I know. There are some poetic glimmers here. The basic elements of concrete poetry are present: the root system for the bud (*knospe*) widens out as it grows, with the words serving as a kind of ideogram. The bud sits askance on a slim stem above branching roots. The visual form and the verbal content enter a different and differential relation. I quite like the "alte[s] erinnern[...]," rendered as the nominalized "old remembering" rather than the more streamlined "old memory," though I might have opted for "aged remembering" to stress the weirdness of the phrase. Good, too, is the "damp with the past" for "feucht vom vergangenen," literally "made moist through things past." Kudos to AI.

Overall, however, ChatGPT does disappoint. The machine uses the adjective "old" twice, once with "old remembering" and a second time with "old stories." The original—if we can call it that—has the multivalent German *Geschichten*, in which a Germanic ear hears both *stories* and *histories*. There is nothing old, aged, or hoary about these buried (hi)stories. My real problem, though, lies with the English verse "roots dig up old stories."* That seems like an unmitigated disaster, a mistake possible only for a beginning German student. The roots are not doing any unearthing. Instead, they are burrowing down, spreading out, forming the large underneath that will give the bud its hidden strength and its heavy baggage as it strains against tomorrow ("vom morgen") as well as the circularity ("der kreis") the last verses suggest.

My little exercise let me breathe a sigh of relief. How good to know that *Good & Safe* has been rendered in English by two skilled translators, Ann Cotten and Anna-Isabella Dinwoodie, attuned to the kinds of nuances the machine cannot yet parse or simulate, for that matter. Ujvary creates instructions, lists, repetition, seriality, and the cybernetic feedback loops we also associate with minimalism and conceptual art of the same period.† We could say the translators provide the next iteration in Ujvary's poetic series, without sacrificing finesse on the altar of probability and statistical averages, with which AI works. The translators' recognition of patterns and relationships within the 1977 book *Sicher & Gut*—and their "update" for our current historical moment—is one the machine cannot copy.

---

* I prefer what DeepL does, which does not quite manage to keep the "rooting" graphic structure of the original:

> bud
> hope
> grows, still
> in the shadow light
> of the old memory
> roots dig stories
> in earth, moist from past
> life. leaves whisper of tomorrow
> that was not yet. a tree, a breath,
> a word. and again the circle begins.

† The special relation between concrete poetry and lists—the fine line between natural and mathematical languages—is described by Ann Cotten: "a series is also a product of a mathematical formula, while a list describes a concrete situation [and] remains pre-mathematical" (in *Nach der Welt: Die Listen der Konkreten Poesie und ihre Folgen*, Wien: Klever, 2008, 88).

Good & Safe is Cotten and Dinwoodie's translation of the German *Sicher & Gut*. With their title, they introduce a hiccup into what seems straightforward. By turning the order of the adjectives around, they play with the platitudes and commonplaces that run like a leitmotif through the collection. It is a bit like the Good & Plenty licorice with which I grew up, widely marketed, a pink and white pleasing to the eye, if not to the palate (the sugarcoating masked a disgusting black licorice on the inside). In Ujvary's poems, declarative statements about the everyday stand side by side, their slight variations forcing us to do a double take. If you turn around a commonsense phrase long enough, you estrange the familiar. If you turn around a commonsense phrase regularly enough, it reveals its ideological underside. If you turn around a commonsense phrase often enough, it reveals the nonsense at its core. The pink or white coating gives way to a black interior. Good & Safe: what is good is not necessarily safe. What is safe is not necessarily good. Goodness and safety hardly go hand in hand.

HOW DO I introduce an experimental writer like Ujvary, little known even among the cognoscenti? Furthermore, how do I introduce such a writer when she is translated by a more famous experimental writer such as Cotten? How do I prevent the translator from overshadowing the poet?

In this case, a good place to start is biography. It reveals themes and throughlines in the poet's oeuvre. Liesl Ujvary was born in 1939 in Bratislava, Slovakia, at the time a clerical fascist client state of Nazi Germany. She has Austrian citizenship and writes in German, but she travels between idioms. She studied Slavic languages as well as art history and ancient Hebrew literature, in both Vienna and Zurich, where she completed her doctorate in 1968. She studied and worked in college and university settings (Zurich, Tokyo, Moscow) until she became a full-time writer in Vienna in 1972. An affinity with dissidents is present in her translations of Soviet poets writing against the state: her anthology *Freedom Is Freedom—Unofficial Soviet*

Poetry, with her own translations of proscribed writers, appeared in 1975 in Zurich. The KGB interviewed Ujvary numerous times during her stay in Moscow, leading to a kind of "grounded paranoia" (see Cotten's afterword), which wends its way through her books. Among Ujvary's myriad publications, several deal with consciousness under pressure, e.g., *Lustige Paranoia* (Funny Paranoia, 1995) and *Das reine Gehirn* (The Pure Brain, 1997). Perhaps as a result of her birth in what was then known as Pressburg, later experiences translating Russian, and living in conservative Austria (which has spawned so many oppositional writers), Ujvary has a fondness for adversarial stances.

Since the 2000s, her interest in consciousness continues as it is impeded, impinged upon, and impelled by our increasingly media-driven and digital world, e.g., in *Kontrollierte Spiele. 7 Artefakte* (Controlled Games: 7 Artefacts, 2002), *Alphaversionen* (Alpha Versions, 2006), and *body & tech* (2023). It may thus come as no surprise that her oeuvre includes experimental electronic music and videos. In all these formats, she allows the multivalent, heteroglossic, and maladjusted to emerge and clash with the normative, univocal, and well-adapted. Computer technology is set against computer technology, as in her experiments with the *trautonium*, an electronic synthesizer that was first invented in the 1930s. The noise is turned up, effective communication is undermined, the hindrances become the stuff of poetry. But the sources of friction, noise, and other disruptive factors are central to *Good & Safe*, her debut from 1977, reissued 40 years later. Today, I assume she enjoys experimenting with AI—and handles its failures with more of a sense of humor than I do.

The Austrian-American poet Ann Cotten (collaborating here with Anna-Isabella Dinwoodie) is an accomplished experimental author in her own right, and she credits Ujvary as a mentor. Cotten's debut, *Fremdwörterbuchsonette* (Foreign Dictionary Sonnets), published by the prestigious Suhrkamp Verlag in 2007, established her as a writer to be reckoned with. Playing with loan words, metrical feet, palindromes, metaphors, and the like, Cotten too is interested in the misinformation and noise that might break open inherited forms such as sonnets. Like Ujvary, she makes the interferences between languages productive and explores various modes of thinking, as readers move between embedded drawings and sonnet-like forms. Words and images become both "false evidence" and "vertiginous indicators" for a world awry and yet oddly stable (Cotten's "Schwindlige Indizien" in that collection activates both meanings). With little collages and drawings in her books, Cotten established herself as a kindred spirit to Ujvary. Her poetological reflections in *Nach der Welt: Die Listen der Konkreten Poesie und ihre Folgen* (After the World: Concrete Poetry's Lists and Their Repercussions, 2008) play with the double meaning of the German noun *Listen*, which can be lists but also feints, tricks, stratagems, and tactics. *Listen* can generate meaning, subvert causality, create humor, indict social norms, and question the parameters of what counts as literature.

In an era where contingency is often elided in favor of a feigned causality, Ujvary stresses how repetition influences the way we perceive the reasons given for things being as they are. Ujvary's lists are an effort to make us think about the conditional nature of most everything—especially our value judgments. This pertains to political issues such as democracy, dictatorship, and governance, as well as to matters of daily life such as traffic, friendship, and consumption. In her poetic permutations, she lists the various opinions regarding social stability and anarchy or revolution. Offering us quirky combinations, she questions whether standard explanations hold. Does full employment lead to prosperity and peace? Or does chaos imply freedom and hence bread and work? What leads to what, and which "various explanations" can we take seriously? In a poem by that title, she asks us to question what is man-made and what God-given, what we need and what we think we need. Another poem entitled "Collected Knowledge" demonstrates that accreted knowledge is as dubious as most appeals to "common sense." Explanations, taken *en masse*, easily tilt into the funny and the absurd. The only thing they explain is our strong desire to give explanations in the face of complex processes that exceed our understanding.

Placing the same statements next to each other, first in the affirmative, then with a negation, she asks us to ponder how we might resolve apparent contradictions. Or not. Where AI simulates reasoning through its algorithmic patterns, her lists, series, and instruction manuals remind us that the philosophical query "What is a good life?" is not easily answered, no matter how straightforward the question—or prompt—and its answer may seem.

Fatima Naqvi
New Haven and Vienna, May 2025

GOOD & SAFE

What Holds the World Together

What Holds the World Together

Tough times — Weak knees
Full breasts — Empty pockets
Hot nights — Cold coffee
Sour grapes — Sweet life
Tight pants — Open hearts
Dear homeland — Cheap flights
Rich harvest — Poor suckers
Big prospects — Small fry
Thin soup — Thick air
Easy women — Heavy weapons
Bright minds — Shady business
Long fingers — Short trial
Old songs — New faces
Unsavory stories — Mellow wine

this is better

democracy is better than dictatorship
butter is better than margarine
schools are better than military training camps
sex is better than booze
humans are better than computers
houses are better than barracks
poems are better than advertisements
students are better than cops
truth is better than lies

this is the same

democracy is like dictatorship
butter is like margarine
schools are like military training camps
sex is like booze
humans are like computers
houses are like barracks
poems are like advertisements
students are like cops
truth is like lies

this has always been like this

democracy has always been like this
butter has always been like this
schools have always been like this
sex has always been like this
humans have always been like this
houses have always been like this
poems have always been like this
students have always been like this
truth has always been like this

there will always be this

there will always be dictatorship
there will always be margarine
there will always be military training camps
there will always be booze
there will always be computers
there will always be barracks
there will always be advertisements
there will always be cops
there will always be lies

Dialectic Objects

The Danube always flows in the same direction.
No, the Danube does not always flow in the same direction.

The new government will be different.
No, the new government will not be different.

The law of gravity is universal.
No, the law of gravity is not universal.

The Communist Party always follows the same principles.
No, the Communist Party does not always follow the same principles.

Politicians like to play with children.
No, politicians do not like to play with children.

A lot can be learned from history.
No, not a lot can be learned from history.

Austria is a neutral country.
No, Austria is not a neutral country.

The sun shines on everyone alike.
No, the sun does not shine on everyone alike.

Military institutions serve national security.
No, military institutions do not serve national security.

At school, children are trained to be citizens.
No, at school, children are not trained to be citizens.

Jesus loves you.
No, Jesus does not love you.

The Burgtheater is an important cultural institution.
No, the Burgtheater is not an important cultural institution.

Capitalism is the best system for society.
No, capitalism is not the best system for society.

The car is a practical means of transportation.
No, the car is not a practical means of transportation.

Art educates.
No, art does not educate.

Our national capital, Vienna, is becoming more beautiful and modern with each passing year.
No, our national capital, Vienna, is not becoming more beautiful and modern with each passing year.

Alcohol is a dangerous poison.
No, alcohol is not a dangerous poison.

More cops means more safety.
No, more cops does not mean more safety.

Collected Knowledge

Yes, it's true that the Danube always flows in the same direction. The Danube always flows in the same direction because we know that the Danube always flows in the same direction.

Yes, it's true that traffic is loud. Traffic is loud because we know that traffic is loud.

Yes, it's true that grapes are sweet. Grapes are sweet because we know that grapes are sweet.

Yes, it's true that the colors of our country are red, white and red. Red, white and red are the colors of our country because we know that red, white and red are the colors of our country.

Yes, it's true that Regina brand kitchens are nice. Regina brand kitchens are nice because we know that Regina brand kitchens are nice.

Yes, it's true that smoking is harmful. Smoking is harmful because we know that smoking is harmful.

Yes, it's true that the Socialist Party is in power. The Socialist Party is in power because we know that the Socialist Party is in power.

Yes, it's true that love brings people together. Love brings people together because we know that love brings people together.

Yes, it's true that coal is expensive. Coal is expensive because we know that coal is expensive.

Yes, it's true that Switzerland shares a border with Austria. Switzerland shares a border with Austria because we know that Switzerland shares a border with Austria.

Yes, it's true that there are military dictatorships in South America. There are military dictatorships in South America because we know that there are military dictatorships in South America.

Yes, it's true that Baader-Meinhof are fighting capitalism. Baader-Meinhof are fighting capitalism because we know that Baader-Meinhof are fighting capitalism.

Yes, it's true that astronauts are exploring outer space. Astronauts are exploring outer space because we know that astronauts are exploring outer space.

Yes, it's true that shopping is fun. Shopping is fun because we know that shopping is fun.

Yes, it's true that the police maintain order. The police maintain order because we know that the police maintain order.

Yes, it's true that air pollution levels are rising. Air pollution levels are rising because we know that air pollution levels are rising.

Yes, it's true that a workweek is 40 hours. A workweek is 40 hours because we know that a workweek is 40 hours.

Yes, it's true that Salzburg is a city of culture. Salzburg is a city of culture because we know that Salzburg is a city of culture.

Yes, it's true that there are bananas in every supermarket. There are bananas in every supermarket because we know that there are bananas in every supermarket.

Yes, it's true that asshole is a curse word. Asshole is a curse word because we know that asshole is a curse word.

Yes, it's true that murderers are criminals. Murderers are criminals because we know that murderers are criminals.

Yes, it's true that the new fashion is exciting. The new fashion is exciting because we know that the new fashion is exciting.

Yes, it's true that Coca-Cola quenches your thirst. Coca-Cola quenches your thirst because we know that Coca-Cola quenches your thirst.

Yes, it's true that green is the color of hope. Green is the color of hope because we know that green is the color of hope.

Yes, it's true that we are free people. We are free people because we know that we are free people.

The Law

Part I / Duties

§ 1 If you have light hair, you must eat what is put on the table.
§ 2 If you fall asleep easily, you must empty your mailbox every day.
§ 3 If you have no children, you must drive your own car to work.
§ 4 If you cut your fingernails short, you must buy rye bread at the bakery.
§ 5 If you wear black pants, you must drink two cups of coffee in the morning.
§ 6 If you tend to gain weight, you must get up at 7:30 on workdays.
§ 7 If you read crime novels, you must live on a busy street.
§ 8 If you go out in the evening, you must dye your hair red.
§ 9 If you have a cold, you must carry coal in winter.
§ 10 If you use a ballpoint pen, you must change your sheets once a week.
§ 11 If you go shopping in the rain, you must write a letter to your parents.
§ 12 If you wear a hat, you must lock your apartment door carefully.
§ 13 If you are building a house, you must limit your caloric intake.
§ 14 If you talk to friends on the telephone, you must replace the typewriter ribbon promptly.
§ 15 If you have natural curls, you must give your neighbors a friendly greeting.
§ 16 If you are fluent in French, you must wear long underwear.
§ 17 If you do not drink alcohol, you must watch TV in the evening.
§ 18 If your teeth hurt, you must go on an excursion over the weekend.
§ 19 If you are registered at your current address, you must take vitamins.
§ 20 If it is your birthday, you must read an independent newspaper.

Part II / Rights

§ 1 If you wear size 40 shoes, you may take a free seat on the tram.
§ 2 If you wear a wristwatch, you may go for a walk in the Stadtpark in spring.
§ 3 If you love classical music, you may have breakfast in the kitchen.
§ 4 If you are successful in your career, you may drink Güssinger mineral water.
§ 5 If you smoke filter cigarettes, you may express your opinion to your friends.
§ 6 If you have finished high school, you may buy laundry detergent and cosmetics.
§ 7 If you travel to Spain in summer, you may do gymnastics every morning.
§ 8 If you are short-sighted, you may attend an English course.
§ 9 If you pay your bills, you may look at the products on display in warehouses.
§ 10 If you have insurance, you may sleep until half past nine on Sundays.
§ 11 If you have a beard, you may look out the window sometimes.
§ 12 If you are unmarried, you may look up a certain number in the telephone book.
§ 13 If you are over 18, you may cross streets at crosswalks.
§ 14 If you do not live on the ground floor, you may go swimming in an indoor pool.
§ 15 If you have blue eyes, you may learn a musical instrument.
§ 16 If you collect stamps, you may open a bank account.
§ 17 If you have stomach problems, you may wear sunglasses in strong sunlight.
§ 18 If you have friends outside the country, you may use artificial sweetener instead of sugar.
§ 19 If you are interested in progress, you may follow all national-league soccer games on TV.

§ 20 If you can spell the word "rhythm," you may take your dog for a walk twice a day.

Security Means Full Employment

I say: Security means full employment
you say: Full employment means affluence
he says: Unemployment means crisis
she says: Crisis means revolution
we say: Revolution means anarchy
you say: Anarchy means fighting
they say: Fighting means war

I say: War means oppression
you say: Oppression means censorship
he says: Censorship means silence
she says: Silence means hate
we say: Hate means fighting
you say: Fighting means upheaval
they say: Upheaval means chaos

I say: Chaos means freedom
you say: Freedom means bread
he says: Bread means work
she says: Work means order
we say: Order means assimilation
you say: Assimilation means compromise
they say: Compromise means illness

I say: Illness means filth
you say: Filth means untidiness
he says: Untidiness means hunger
she says: Hunger means unemployment
we say: Unemployment means crisis
you say: Crisis means unrest
they say: Unrest means upheaval

I say:	Upheaval means revolution
you say:	Revolution means freedom
he says:	Freedom means independence
she says:	Independence means affluence
we say:	Affluence means full employment
you say:	Full employment means work
they say:	Work means force

I say:	Force means violence
you say:	Violence means torture
he says:	Torture means dictatorship
she says:	Dictatorship means lack of freedom
we say:	Lack of freedom means work
you say:	Work means affluence
they say:	Affluence means security

March of the Natural Numbers

one
two
three
four
five
six
seven
eight
nine
ten

ten eggs
ten children
ten cities
ten people
ten computers
ten books
ten soldiers
ten bottles

ten fresh eggs
ten austrian children
ten megacities
ten black people
ten IBM computers
ten beautiful women
ten private cars
ten textbooks

ten brave soldiers
ten liquor bottles

ten fresh eggs cost 17 schillings
ten austrian children learn multiplication
ten megacities drown in smog
ten black people were given no say
ten IBM computers control the city administration
ten beautiful women smile from the billboard
ten private cars are parked in front of the house
ten textbooks teach mathematics
ten brave soldiers defend the fatherland
ten liquor bottles are downed

Various Explanations

pleasure comes from work
dust comes from cleaning
streets come from traffic
books come from reading
wine comes from drinking
weapons come from the enemy
nonsense comes from reason
the church comes from faith
borders come from other countries

pleasure comes from god
dust comes from god
streets comes from god
books come from god
wine comes from god
weapons come from god
nonsense comes from god
the church comes from god
borders come from god

pleasure comes from the economic system
dust comes from the economic system
streets come from the economic system
books come from the economic system
wine comes from the economic system
weapons come from the economic system
nonsense comes from the economic system
the church comes from the economic system
borders come from the economic system

no pleasure—no work
no dust—no cleaning
no streets—no traffic
no books—no reading
no wine—no drinking
no weapons—no enemies
no nonsense—no reason
no church—no faith
no borders—no other countries

we need work
we need cleaning
we need traffic
we need reading
we need drinking
we need the enemy
we need reason
we need faith
we need other countries

we are against pleasure
we are against dust
we are against streets
we are against books
we are against wine
we are against weapons
we are against nonsense
we are against the church
we are against borders

Anticommunists are against communists. If you are antiamerican and anticommunist, you are against America and against communists. If you are anticlerical, antiamerican and anticommunist, you are against the church, against America and against communists. If you are antisemitic, anticlerical, antiamerican and anticommunist, you are against Jews, against the church, against America and against communists. If you are antifascist, antisemitic, anticlerical, antiamerican and anticommunist, you are against fascists, against Jews, against the church, against America and against communists. If you are antiimperialist, antifascist, antisemitic, anticlerical, antiamerican and anticommunist, you are against imperialists, against fascists, against Jews, against the church, against America and against communists. If you are antisoviet, antiimperialist, antifascist, antisemitic, anticlerical, antiamerican and anticommunist, you are against the Soviets, against imperialists, against fascists, against Jews, against the church, against America and against communists. If you are antiauthoritarian, antisoviet, antiimperialist, antifascist, antisemitic, anticlerical, antiamerican and anticommunist, you are against authoritarians, against the Soviets, against imperialists, against fascists, against Jews, against the church, against America and against communists.

untitled

this is mine
and this is yours
and this is his
and this is hers
and this is theirs

i give you nothing
and you give me nothing
and he gives her nothing
and we give you nothing
and you give us nothing
and they give them nothing

This Is Wrong!

The face should not be ugly.
The eyes should not be swollen.
The gaze should not be shifty and dull.
The cheeks should not be wrinkled and gray.
The nose should not be bent.
The lips should not be pale and dry.
The chin should not be soft.
The hair should not be lank, thin, brittle and colorless.
The skin should not be cracked, reddened, oily and rough.
The neck should not be short and fat.
The shoulders should not be slumped.
The armpits should not be sweaty.
The arms should not be thin and scrawny.
The joints should not be bony.
The hands should not be rough and moist.
The fingers should not be thick and clumsy.
The fingertips should not be hard.
The fingernails should not be chewed and dirty.
The breast should not be small, limp, droopy and sunken.
The belly should not be large and flabby.
The hips should not be wide.
The butt cheeks should not be fat and wobbly.
The thighs should not be weak and heavy.
The knees should not be pointy.
The shins should not be crooked.
The calves should not be thick.
The ankles should not be plump.
The feet should not be big and misshapen.

This Is Right!

The face should be beautiful.
The eyes should be clear.
The gaze should be candid and radiant.
The cheeks should be full and rosy.
The nose should be straight.
The lips should be red and moist.
The chin should be energetic.
The hair should be smooth and supple.
The skin should be white, clean and velvety.
The neck should be slim and graceful.
The shoulders should be broad and strong.
The armpits should be dry.
The arms should be round and full.
The joints should be delicate.
The hands should be soft.
The fingers should be slim and flexible.
The fingertips should be sensitive.
The fingernails should be manicured.
The breast should be taut, full, plump and smooth.
The belly should be firm.
The hips should be high.
The butt cheeks should be small and firm.
The thighs should be strong.
The knees should be round.
The shins should be straight.
The calves should be slim.
The ankles should be dainty.
The feet should be small and well-shaped.

A Little Advice for Life

Your blanket makes ugly little wrinkles when you brush against it accidentally. Stroke it lightly with the palm of your hand and the blanket will be smooth again.

During meals, breadcrumbs, grains of rice, bits of noodles or a strip of sausage skin drop to the ground and stick in an unappetizing manner. Take a moist cloth and wipe the ground carefully after every meal.

It is unbearably hot in your apartment. You are thirsty, thirsty, thirsty! Turn on the faucet and drink a glass of cold, clear water.

The mail carrier brings you advertisements, flyers, catalogs almost every day. Throw this bulk mail into the garbage after you read it.

After three or four days, your underwear starts to emit an unpleasant smell. Wash yourself thoroughly and put on fresh underwear.

Your eyes hurt and tear up from watching TV for hours. With a touch of the button, the TV is off and your eyes can rest.

Your suit looks shabby, the sleeves have rubbed off, the pants are shiny and have spots. Go to a department store and buy a new suit.

You are interested in everything around you. Read newspapers, listen to the radio, watch TV, keep your eyes and ears open.

You want to leave the city, urban life is making you ill. Go to the ticket counter at the nearest train station, buy a ticket to a destination of your choice and board the train.

When you go for a walk, pieces of gravel fall into your shoes. Stop for a moment and empty your shoes.

You get strong headaches from unpleasant family discussions. Take an aspirin with some water and lie down to rest for a quarter of an hour.

You cannot sleep, the tiniest noise startles you. Close all the windows and doors and wait for sleep to come.

When you have errands in town, you meet people you would rather not see. Look away and pretend you don't recognize them.

You can never make your money last to the end of the month. Write down all expenses precisely and economize where you can.

You dislike being alone in the evening. Call a friend and spend the evening in pleasant company.

Greasy, heavy cooking makes you feel sick to your stomach. Drink a shot of schnaps and your stomach will be alright.

You are not a morning person, you feel ill and weak after getting up. Drink two cups of strong coffee and you will wake up.

Your back hurts from typing. Do morning exercises routinely and your back muscles will loosen up.

Relatives and acquaintances ask about your well-being every time you meet. Answer their questions with "fine, thanks."

You're annoyed about a negative answer you have received. Light a cigarette and your nerves will calm down.

The telephone rings all day at your house. Lift up the receiver and say your name.

Your apartment is untidy and dirty. Put everything in its place and clean thoroughly.

You like nature. Take a walk in the park.

You are hungry. Eat!

You are cold. Put on some clothes!

You are tired. Go to sleep!

You are lonely. Get married!

You are ill. Go to the doctor!

You are afraid. Lock the door!

fully programmed (1)

he stretches
he gets up
he washes and shaves
he drinks coffee
he reads the paper
he goes to work
he greets his colleagues
he works
he eats lunch
he works
he goes home
he greets his wife
he eats bread cheese and sausage
he drinks wine
he watches tv
he gets undressed and goes to sleep
he stretches
he gets up

fully programmed (2)

she stretches
she gets up
she makes coffee
she gets dressed
she takes the child away
she goes shopping
she reads the paper
she eats lunch
she cleans and irons
she picks the child up
she gets supper ready
she eats bread cheese and sausage
she drinks wine
she watches tv
she gets undressed and washes
she goes to sleep
she stretches
she gets up

Peter Stuyvesant Goes on a Journey

In Vienna the sky is blue
In Rome the sky is blue
In New Orleans the sky is blue
In Tokyo the sky is blue

In Vienna there are streets and squares
In Rome there are streets and squares
In New Orleans there are streets and squares
In Tokyo there are streets and squares

In Vienna you meet beautiful women
In Rome you meet beautiful women
In New Orleans you meet beautiful women
In Tokyo you meet beautiful women

In Vienna they drink Scotch
In Rome they drink Scotch
In New Orleans they drink Scotch
In Tokyo they drink Scotch

In Vienna jet planes take off and touch down
In Rome jet planes take off and touch down
In New Orleans jet planes take off and touch down
In Tokyo jet planes take off and touch down

"Have a taste"

Wieners
Tyrolers
French
Hamburgers
Frankfurters
Ulmers
Göttingers
Parisians
Florentines
Lüneburgers
Braunschweigers
Leipzigers
Augsburgers
Westphalians
Thüringers
Linzers
Ischlers
Wachauers
Waldviertlers
Praguers
Boers
Krakauers
Bosniaks
Debreziners
Kranskies
Beskadas
Indians
Eskimos
Russians

the lovely city
dedicated to all the men and women of vienna

vienna is dead
vienna's ahead
vienna's fun
vienna's done
vienna's fast-paced
vienna's a rat race
vienna rises
vienna's in crisis
vienna's slow
vienna's a freak show
vienna's rusting
vienna's disgusting
vienna's rooted
vienna's polluted
vienna's sick
vienna's a dick
vienna's rewarding
vienna's boring
vienna's driving
vienna's arriving
vienna's endearing
vienna's disappearing
vienna's alive
vienna's a bee hive
vienna's a blight
vienna's alright
vienna's undying
vienna's buying
vienna polishes
vienna demolishes
vienna's sinking

vienna's shrinking
vienna unites
vienna violates human rights
vienna's greedy
vienna's seedy
vienna, death's kiss
vienna exists

the lovely city
dedicated to bodo hell and thomas bernhard

salzburg is dead
salzburg's ahead
salzburg's fun
salzburg's done
salzburg's fast-paced
salzburg's a rat race
salzburg rises
salzburg's in crisis
salzburg's slow
salzburg's a freak show
salzburg's rusting
salzburg's disgusting
salzburg's rooted
salzburg's polluted
salzburg's sick
salzburg's a dick
salzburg's rewarding
salzburg's boring
salzburg's driving
salzburg's arriving
salzburg's endearing
salzburg's disappearing
salzburg's alive
salzburg's a bee hive
salzburg's a blight
salzburg's alright
salzburg's undying
salzburg's buying
salzburg polishes
salzburg demolishes
salzburg's sinking

salzburg's shrinking
salzburg unites
salzburg violates human rights
salzburg's greedy
salzburg's seedy
salzburg, death's kiss
salzburg exists

the lovely city
for the writers' association of graz

graz is dead
graz's ahead
graz's fun
graz's done
graz's fast-paced
graz's a rat race
graz rises
graz's in crisis
graz's slow
graz's a freak show
graz's rusting
graz's disgusting
graz's rooted
graz's polluted
graz's sick
graz's a dick
graz's rewarding
graz's boring
graz's driving
graz's arriving
graz's endearing
graz's disappearing
graz's alive
graz's a bee hive
graz's a blight
graz's alright
graz's undying
graz's buying
graz polishes
graz demolishes
graz's sinking

graz's shrinking
graz unites
graz violates human rights
graz's greedy
graz's seedy
graz, death's kiss
graz exists

the lovely city
to austrian writers abroad

berlin is dead
berlin's ahead
berlin's fun
berlin's done
berlin's fast-paced
berlin's a rat race
berlin rises
berlin's in crisis
berlin's slow
berlin's a freak show
berlin's rusting
berlin's disgusting
berlin's rooted
berlin's polluted
berlin's sick
berlin's a dick
berlin's rewarding
berlin's boring
berlin's driving
berlin's arriving
berlin's endearing
berlin's disappearing
berlin's alive
berlin's a bee hive
berlin's a blight
berlin's alright
berlin's undying
berlin's buying
berlin polishes
berlin demolishes
berlin's sinking

berlin's shrinking
berlin unites
berlin violates human rights
berlin's greedy
berlin's seedy
berlin, death's kiss
berlin exists

the lovely city
to vagrich bakhchanyan and all people in new york

new york is dead
new york's ahead
new york's fun
new york's done
new york's fast-paced
new york's a rat race
new york rises
new york's in crisis
new york's slow
new york's a freak show
new york's rusting
new york's disgusting
new york's rooted
new york's polluted
new york's sick
new york's a dick
new york's rewarding
new york's boring
new york's driving
new york's arriving
new york's endearing
new york's disappearing
new york's alive
new york's a bee hive
new york's a blight
new york's alright
new york's undying
new york's buying
new york polishes
new york demolishes
new york's sinking

new york's shrinking
new york unites
new york violates human rights
new york's greedy
new york's seedy
new york, death's kiss
new york exists

Do You Not Sense Anything?

Do You Not Sense Anything?

The human body is covered in skin. The skin can be sliced open. Under the skin is . . . something.

In the walls along the street there are dark doorways. In the doorways is . . . something.

Central Europeans walk in shoes. Under the shoes is . . . something.

Without water, there is no life. Once used, the water flows into the drain. Inside the drain is . . . something.

In this building, there are many doors. On door No. 29 a sign reads "Schweizer." Behind the door is . . . something.

A bridge spans the gorge. Under the bridge is . . . something.

City dwellers like to go for walks in the park, where there are trees and benches. In the treetops is . . . something.

The oral cavity is moist and warm. The tongue lies inside the oral cavity. People can touch each other with their tongues. Inside the mouth is . . . something.

The supermarket is brightly lit. Confectioner's sugar, white beans, puff pastry, Milupa infant formula, coffee, Gösser beer and many other goods are on display. Inside the packaging is . . . something.

Helga has a narrow face and brown eyes. In her eyes is . . . something.

Solitary cars drive through the city at night. The traffic light at the intersection changes from red to yellow to green and from green to yellow to red. In the middle of the intersection is . . . something.

Surprising Similarities

a face like a belly
a belly like a gas stove
a gas stove like a tulip
a tulip like a cow
a cow like packing paper
packing paper like a wet towel
a wet towel like a loaf of bread
a loaf of bread like a kiss
a kiss like a spruce tree
a spruce tree like a tablespoon
a tablespoon like a stovepipe
a stovepipe like a teardrop
a teardrop like car exhaust
car exhaust like coffee creamer
coffee creamer like rusty nails
rusty nails like a headrest
a headrest like a pair of pants
a pair of pants like a sunset
a sunset like rain boots
rain boots like Emmentaler cheese
Emmentaler cheese like a patch of snow
a patch of snow like a face

Secret Contact

window touching door
door touching floor
floor touching carpet
carpet touching leather sole
leather sole touching stocking
stocking touching skin
skin touching bread
bread touching china
china touching fish
fish touching glass
glass touching wire
wire touching plastic
plastic touching stone
stone touching earth
earth touching asphalt
asphalt touching concrete
concrete touching meadow
meadow touching concrete
concrete touching plaster
plaster touching sand
sand touching brick
brick touching window
window touching hand
hand touching chin
chin touching mouth
mouth touching chocolate
chocolate touching paper
paper touching ashtray
ashtray touching cigarette
cigarette touching mouth
mouth touching cigarette
cigarette touching toilet

toilet touching shit
shit touching bowel
bowel touching pepper
pepper touching lamb
lamb touching pork
pork touching beef
beef touching knife
knife touching board
board touching Formica
Formica touching zinc sheet
zinc sheet touching red wine
red wine touching white wine
white wine touching whiskey
whiskey touching coffee
coffee touching roll
roll touching sausage
sausage touching beer
beer touching schnaps
schnaps touching glass
glass touching hand
hand touching pencil
pencil touching pocket
pocket touching key
key touching photo
photo touching money
money touching wool
wool touching private parts
private parts touching bedsheet
bedsheet touching mattress
mattress touching floor

three true stories

first true story

the fence is a window and the window is a room and the room is a table and the table is a speck and the speck is a girl and the girl is a knife and the knife is a clock and the clock is a letter and the letter is a neighbor and the neighbor is a flowerbed and the flowerbed is a city and the city is a street and the street is a friend and the friend is a summer's day and the summer's day is a hill and the hill is a field and the field is a tower and the tower is a woman and the woman is a wave and the wave is glasses and the glasses are an evening and the evening is a tree and the tree is a mound and the mound is a key and the key is a coin and the coin is a sheet of ice and the sheet of ice is a hole and the hole is a bridge and the bridge is a pillar and the pillar is a look and the look is a colleague and the colleague is a stick and the stick is a mountain and the mountain is a journey and the journey is a café and the café is a camp and the camp is a wolfhound and the wolfhound is a grate and the grate is an abyss and the abyss is a toilet and the toilet is a school

second true story

the gesture
becomes a friend
becomes a table
becomes feet
becomes cigarettes
becomes laughter
becomes a threat
becomes wine
becomes a map of the city
becomes the cold
becomes running
becomes pavement
becomes an entryway
becomes a man
becomes a society
becomes silence
becomes dirt
becomes escape
becomes a boyfriend
becomes music on the radio
becomes a headache
becomes a car
becomes a child
becomes a rustling
becomes a corridor
becomes an invoice
becomes an encyclopedia
becomes a frame
becomes a parquet floor
becomes a professor
becomes a boulder
becomes chocolate

becomes wall-to-wall carpeting

becomes traffic noise

becomes sunshine

becomes a television

becomes back pain

becomes a Yugoslavian woman

becomes a cornfield

becomes a bottle of aftershave

becomes a pond

becomes a pill

becomes a goodbye

becomes a pair of shoes

becomes a telephone conversation

third true story

horse has head
head has hat
hat has mouth
mouth has face
face has woman
woman has skirt
skirt has lump
lump has child
child has wagon
wagon has bird
bird has tree
tree has stick
stick has arm
arm has suit
suit has hole
hole has wound
wound has eye
eye has fur
fur has leg
leg has fruit
fruit has beak
beak has knife
knife has neck
neck has dog
dog has chain
chain has house
house has wheels
wheels have rope
rope has apple
apple has cave
cave has fence
fence has ravine

ravine has waterfall
waterfall has hands
hands have roots
roots have noses
noses have bruises
bruises have pastures
pastures have ants
ants have rider
rider has horse

instants

instant (1)

the knife, gripped by its handle, cutting edge set along the side of the onion, is drawn firmly through from top to bottom

instant (2)

the road runs through the valley ... the forested slopes rise and fall ... branches whip in the wind ... the stream rushes to the valley floor ... mountains stretch into the distance ... a large scree field approaches the valley ... dustclouds swell

instant (3)

setting: A-6370 kitzbühel, klausnerfeld 3
may 9, 1974, 10 a.m.
partly cloudy, 16°C

first floor: frau stöckl in the kitchen (washing)
frau engel in the kitchen (cooking)
frau zwicknagl in the bathroom (washing)
frau beisl in the bedroom (making the beds)

second floor: frau maier in the kitchen (cleaning vegetables)
frau thurner on the balcony (watering the flowers)
frau pacher on the balcony (reading the paper)
frau haid in the kitchen (cooking)

third floor: herr schiechtl in bed (smoking)
               herr pletzer in the kitchen (eating breakfast)
               frau müller in the kitchen (cooking)
               frau mader in bed (has the flu)

note:
1. there is no one in the building besides the people mentioned
2. each person mentioned is alone in a room
3. the people mentioned are unable to communicate with one another

the fat sausage

the bed is too narrow
the chair is too high
the oven is too hot
the dress is too tight
the floor is too cold
the light is too bright
the road is too long
the milk is too sweet
the street is too dusty
the forest is too dense
the ground is too damp
the mountain is too steep
the coat is too warm
the rock is too heavy
the socks are too thick
the room is too small
the window is too big
the walls are too thin
the cheese is too mild
the bread is too dry
the sausage is too fat
the wine is too strong
the radio is too loud
the shoes are too light
the meadow is too wet
the houses are too tall
the meat is too expensive
the night is too long
the weather is too inconsistent
the tea is too bitter
time is too short

but first then oh come on another one of the same please he's just so awkward yes maybe i guess that could be worth a try mhm that's fine too may i just quickly this is what it's about well actually nothing at all who even started this is complicated in any case by tomorrow morning i absolutely need another shot you got it herbert's sitting over there which herbert i don't know him can we do anything about it he's just so insecure no self-confidence first of all he's looking for a girl which of course is the wrong he's so nice and intelligent but not when are you going on saturday i'm going sunday anyway which of course just the thing for the depressed and suicidal there aren't any why they're already dead but there are a ton of people who could still be helped one more of these please now i'm doing significantly better can i give you two a couple invitations for what of course you're the one from IBM i know i remember perfectly were you there then no i only know he was completely wasted and then rolled up in a rug times just one moment in that closet and so on a couple blonde girls i can imagine but it drives you crazy every now and then not very often i can't stand him at all his style he must every time **we can't get out** i always order puntigamer and i always get schwechater did you know that puntigamer the main thing is not to hurt each other or have any emotional he can drink himself to death for all i no not at the moment that doesn't matter well you can always set something up lack of sleep icy streets hey look i have a big favor to ask well what is it either you buy it or you lend it to me sometime those are huge obstacles next to the freeway on top of a hill well gentlemen yes just a minute and then probably gets frustrated because he says he's coming and then he doesn't come odd yes and throwing all that money down the drain the main thing is she's fed up now would be good to eat something but where eggs with bacon that's not the current status anymore anyway doesn't matter may i just really quickly not a long distance call again unfortunately i'm running a little late how are you in two three hours alright alright now we'll wrap that up nicely show me here you go twenty schillings no way that's for the next one too drink another cup of tea and write it down if not it's your own fault on the second me on the fifteenth again why did you go today no not today but yes then one more time i still have to here we are i live here in are you getting out let's go home well then at home we can still have a good one that's an idea so much gets lost yes he was there and i felt so bad for the longest time i didn't get it from who did you say anything to anybody no nobody until four thirty that night we were still he was really interested write it down i have ten days so little little a lot there do i do that again then that and no no more geology but it's all so much and so that is called mother rock he has no idea what he should do with himself and if it says geographic institute of the university he opens it i just yelled and banged my fist on the glass he can just say i'm not there he's having a nervous breakdown and that's it send my regards i cough and cough wherever i touch everything hurts now i take these pills and drink a syrup but i think the pills get you down even more don't go outside today because the weather's cold and drizzly anyway and that's so irritating at my place you know the wood stove is in the other room it's just from him of all people i wouldn't expect something like that but who cares now what are you doing a lot the fact that i'm even here well i said yes very pleasant i like the kids especially the two little ones come let's eat now great everything so good i could stay all night we haven't talked at all i didn't talk to anyone wiener neustadt maybe yes why not oh dear in february it's so cold it was so stressful because her mother died a couple days ago seventy one had bad eyesight for twenty years and surgery too for age-related stuff everything you can imagine yeah lapses of consciousness **we're in here** depression aggression on the twenty third we had an appointment but she couldn't make it heart attack a lot but not expensive a kilogram something about that much that's for me and i'll take one along on monday i'll call you don't know about the key after two thirty i'll be there did you guys like it very good walter would have liked to stay all night he's dangerous but not at all why did he go then everyone told me i don't know what's wrong with me i can't do this kind of thing anymore i have to talk to you is it urgent do you need to go somewhere i would like to meet people who are a little older not only problems with men all the time i like to be trusting but there a light goes on if then no eva was also thirty-two would like to have one or two more kids you know i'm on the pill you have so many corrective mechanisms can she really take you to task if so then so what if you need me anytime today maybe before nine anyway not good then a little later a bottle or two just tell me quickly the number in the apartment everything's falling apart if it's not the drain it's that and the needle on the record player is broken too the day before yesterday the gas bill but for now i'm still waiting the two hundred dollars he's so impulsive you just can't really know give my regards to both of them please she just lay down the day after tomorrow we fly all the suitcases and boxes that's why we always look as fast as possible maybe we can do it in the spring it's all in the letter i wrote it down for you PO box five oh oh one five oh oh give everyone my love and talk everyone out of it's like a leap and what comes after exceptions sit down went by there today the house on aschbachweg down by the creek is already finished too back by frau spitzer's where the harisch family lives back there a nice house not too big a couple people already living not all of them the others at kaps castle the groundwater has been drained now look very nice five or six big houses wide the garages underneath of course concrete everywhere in the parking lots can't really call it nice why not at all some have christmas trees on the balcony the location is wonderful well and out back they have the golf course at least no buildings no driveway nothing yes actually primarily germans come from munich or somewhere two three hours no by train less for the people from the big city i understand that get out for once away from it all nature is always nice can you imagine what that means on lebenberg too the one at the bend will be done soon very well built with wood and natural stone round very big windows and a fireplace inside right next to it the three-story one probably ten apartments right next to each other true but there's not so much space and it has to be used they aren't allowed to build any higher private houses no more than three stories except of course hotels everything protected with fiber cement paneling the foundations were a problem in the swampy meadow farther up it's pretty damp too but everything was filled up with concrete so close together view anyway the concrete in front the ice rink out back the noise and the music all day built really cheap they were the ones from east tyrol you could see from the window frames when the plaster wasn't on yet was anybody for it **we can't get in** who would pay so much for it running into the millions but there are always people even there people already living not even possible anymore the streets are just too narrow for those big cars not used to it either the mountains don't know winter and get stuck of course chop down the trees and it'll be wider on the road to the lake as well in one night all chopped down there are supposed to be new ones planted and who's walking nowadays everyone goes by car air mattresses chairs or skis so heavy to carry out of that synthetic resin and then the high boots too now can barely walk they're digging in the field next to the palffy house probably will be apartments too they need money cause they want to build so that's why they're selling land if you don't expand the economy needs it otherwise everything comes to a standstill what will they do lots of them are realizing now

medical history

somebody reads the menu somebody sits and talks somebody dodges the tram fare somebody wants to visit somebody somebody makes a phone call somebody talks somebody drinks white wine somebody drinks tea somebody is tired and wants to sleep somebody reads a book and thinks of somebody somebody sweats somebody wants coffee somebody wants to go for a walk somebody goes to the vending machine and buys cigarettes somebody wants to eat nuts somebody eats braised beef and broth and bread somebody writes a letter somebody turns on the radio and listens to the news somebody eats grapes somebody goes to the bathroom somebody combs their hair somebody tucks themselves in with a blanket somebody asks about somebody somebody answers somebody walks through the pedestrian zone somebody waits for somebody somebody sends their regards to somebody somebody gets a call somebody is tired somebody is sick somebody goes on an excursion somebody looks at the evening sky somebody wants to stay here somebody is worried somebody has a birthday somebody has a nightmare and wakes up bathed in sweat somebody can't stand loud noises somebody has to go to tyrol somebody curses somebody takes the elevator down to the basement somebody is afraid at night somebody cooks rice somebody is short-sighted somebody shivers somebody leaves somebody laughs who laughs who leaves who shivers who is short-sighted who cooks rice who is afraid at night who takes the elevator down to the basement who curses who has to go to tyrol who can't stand loud noises who has a nightmare and wakes up bathed in sweat who has a birthday who is worried who wants to stay here who looks at the evening sky who goes on an excursion who is sick who is tired who gets a call who sends their regards to whom who waits for whom who walks through the pedestrian zone who answers who asks about whom who tucks themselves in with a blanket who combs their hair who goes to the bathroom who eats grapes who turns on the radio and listens to the news who writes a letter who eats braised beef and broth and bread who wants to eat nuts who goes to the vending machine and buys cigarettes who wants to go for a walk who wants coffee who sweats who reads a book and thinks of whom who is tired and wants to sleep who drinks tea who drinks white wine who talks who makes a phone call who wants to visit whom who dodges the fare on the tram who sits and talks who reads the menu nobody reads the menu nobody sits and talks nobody dodges the fare on the tram nobody wants to visit anybody nobody makes a phone call nobody talks nobody drinks white wine nobody drinks tea nobody is tired and wants to sleep nobody reads a book and thinks of anybody nobody sweats nobody wants coffee nobody wants to go for a walk nobody goes to the vending machine and buys cigarettes nobody wants to eat nuts nobody eats braised beef and broth and bread nobody writes a letter nobody turns on the radio and listens to the news nobody eats grapes nobody goes to the bathroom nobody combs their hair nobody tucks themselves in with a blanket nobody asks about anybody nobody answers nobody walks through the pedestrian zone nobody waits for anybody nobody sends their regards to anybody nobody gets a call nobody is tired nobody is sick nobody goes on an excursion nobody looks at the evening sky nobody wants to stay here nobody is worried nobody has a birthday nobody has a nightmare and wakes up bathed in sweat nobody can't stand loud noises nobody has to go to tyrol nobody curses nobody takes the elevator down to the basement nobody is afraid at night nobody cooks rice nobody is short-sighted nobody shivers nobody leaves nobody laughs everybody laughs everybody leaves everybody shivers everybody is short-sighted everybody cooks rice everybody is afraid at night everybody takes the elevator down to the basement everybody curses everybody has to go to tyrol everybody can't stand loud noises everybody has a nightmare and wakes up bathed in sweat everybody has a birthday everybody is worried everybody wants to stay here everybody looks at the evening sky everybody goes on an excursion everybody is sick everybody is tired everybody gets a call everybody sends their regards to everybody everybody waits for everybody everybody walks through the pedestrian zone everybody answers everybody asks about everybody everybody tucks themselves in with a blanket everybody combs their hair everybody goes to the bathroom everybody eats grapes everybody turns on the radio and listens to the news everybody writes a letter everybody eats braised beef and broth and bread everybody wants to eat nuts everybody goes to the vending machine and buys cigarettes everybody wants to go for a walk everybody wants coffee everybody sweats everybody reads a book and thinks of everybody everybody is tired and wants to sleep everybody drinks tea everybody drinks white wine everybody talks everybody makes a phone call everybody wants to visit everybody everybody dodges the fare on the tram everybody sits and talks everybody reads the menu

A Bloodbath

Herbert saw Paul.
A lot of people know me.
Today I ran into Frau Schweizer.
It is Monday, October 8, 1975.
French literature is interesting.
This apple tastes sour.
It's late.
We're coming to visit you.
These people are talking to each other now.
The doctor says: You're sick.
The greengrocer's grandson is called Thomas.
Teeth should be brushed every day.
Frau Holaubek is beautiful.
Herr Professor Wehrli is right.
The Social Democrats won the absolute majority again.
Old buildings are demolished.
Yesterday it was cool and rainy.
After work we have a meal.
This black coat is mine.
This coat is dirty.
How are you? Fine.
How's your son? Also fine.
Peter loves Brigitte.
You can reach Toni.
What would you like? A quarter pound of baloney.
The mailman brings the mail.
The garbage collection takes the trash.
The police work day and night for our safety.
Paul Pabst lives.
Yes, you!

fatalities

father
mother
brother
sister
daughter
son
uncle
aunt
niece
nephew
cousin
sister-in-law
brother-in-law
grandson
granddaughter
grandfather
grandmother

great authorizations

you may be expected to
you may be able to
you may be required to
you may be allowed to

you may be expected to be expected to
you may be able to be expected to
you may be required to be expected to
you may be allowed to be expected to

you may be expected to be able to
you may be able to be able to
you may be required to be able to
you may be allowed to be able to

you may be expected to be required to
you may be able to be required to
you may be required to be required to
you may be allowed to be required to

you may be expected to be allowed to
you may be able to be allowed to
you may be required to be allowed to
you may be allowed to be allowed to

you may be expected to be expected to be expected to
you may be able to be able to be expected to
you may be required to be required to be expected to
you may be allowed to be allowed to be expected to

you may be expected to be expected to be able to
you may be able to be able to be able to
you may be required to be required to be able to
you may be allowed to be allowed to be able to

you may be expected to be expected to be required to
you may be able to be able to be required to
you may be required to be required to be required to
you may be allowed to be allowed to be required to

you may be expected to be expected to be allowed to
you may be able to be able to be allowed to
you may be required to be required to be allowed to
you may be allowed to be allowed to be allowed to

That's an Order!

Do you want to eat?
Do you want to see?
Do you want to learn?
Do you want to drink?
Do you want to sleep?
Do you want to work?
Do you want to live?
Do you want to go?
Do you want to take?
Do you want to forget?
Do you want to believe?
Do you want to give?
Do you want to read?
Do you want to hope?
Do you want to scream?
Do you want to love?
Do you want to order?
Do you want to speak?

Accepted Assertions

We are said to be happy.
I think we are happy.
Butter is said to be healthy.
I think butter is healthy.
Women are said to be different from men.
I think women are different from men.
Grass is said to be green.
I think grass is green.
All people are said to be equal.
I think all people are equal.
Smoking is said to be harmful.
I think smoking is harmful.
God is said to exist.
I think God exists.
Work is said to be necessary.
I think work is necessary.
Cancer is said to be incurable.
I think cancer is incurable.
Language is said to serve communication.
I think language serves communication.

There's a Reason for Everything

Beer gives you a beer belly.
If you work hard and save up, you can buy a nice kitchen.
Women have children.
The streets empty out when it rains.
Cars are convenient. They contaminate the air.
Chile is now ruled by a military dictatorship.
One and one is two.
In this country anyone can make something of themselves. If you can't do anything, you won't amount to anything.
If you sow wheat, wheat is what you get.
The driver was lucky and got away with minor injuries.
A crime of passion.
Yugoslavians meet up at the Südbahnhof.
UFO research in the United States is a secret.
The military serves national defense.
The traffic regulations.

leave it as it is

the government is governing
the sidewalk is dusty
austria is a neutral country
the forest is being clear-cut
grammar is applied
the workers respectfully greet the supervisor
on escalators, the rule is: walk on the left, stand on the right
citizens' rights are limited
women adore *Triumph*™
liberty is indivisible
some people swear each other eternal love
Almliesl homogenized milk keeps for three months
tomorrow is tuesday, october 8, 1974
lunch today is potatoes and blood sausage
weeds are growing waist-high in the garden
the dishes are dirty
in the wardrobe there are 2 towels and 1 shirt

it's all here

a mattress for sleeping, a glass for drinking, other glasses, an inn, a waitress, coffee and beer, younger men, a drag queen with a dog, traffic lights, cigarette machines, bus stops, schnaps, long-distance walls, a door, rows of low houses, afternoons and evenings, money, other places to eat, freeways, train stations, pants and skirts, fountains, cops, tedious stretches, bookstores, orange juice, a typewriter, words, crime novels, conversations on the phone, a sausage, beer and wine, goodbyes, suicide, sleep, left, right, straight ahead, a letter, a thought, a parking lot, rocks, an empty riverbank, cars, the mortgage bank, the people's bank, a grassy area, trees, bushes, sidewalks, traffic lanes, large cold rooms, coffee, mineral water, suggestions, conversations, condiments, industrial wineries, fast-food restaurants, fees, help, foreigners, cannons, atom bombs, ovens

Poems About Poems

love song

who'll stay with me through thick and thin
who'll traipse through town with me all night
who'll sing with me in bright sunshine
who'll drink with me the summer wine

oh stay with me through thick and thin
oh traipse through town with me all night
oh sing with me in bright sunshine
oh drink with me the summer wine

you alone stay with me through thick and thin
you alone traipse through town with me all night
you alone sing with me in bright sunshine
you alone drink with me the summer wine

together we stay through thick and thin
together we traipse through town all night
together we sing in bright sunshine
together we drink the summer wine

who is that staying through thick and thin
who is that traipsing through town all night
who is that singing in bright sunshine
who is that drinking the summer wine

we keep staying and staying through thick and thin
we keep traipsing and traipsing through town all night
we keep singing and singing in bright sunshine
we keep drinking and drinking the summer wine

who'll stay with me through thick and thin
who'll traipse through town with me all night
who'll sing with me in bright sunshine
who'll drink with me the summer wine

marching song

this is dark and that is light
this is day and that is night
this is hot and that is cold
this is new and that is old

this is above and that's below
this is deep and that is shallow
this is a little and that's a lot
this is cold and that is hot

this is up and that is down
this has corners that is round
this is sick and that is healthy
this is poor and that is wealthy

this is black and that is red
this is living that is dead
this is truth and that is falsehood
this is bad and that is good

mood poem

the cranes migrate
the autumn wind blows
the hair is windswept
the streets are empty
the inn is bright
the air is smoky
the mood is good

autumn poem

I want to write an autumn poem
I want to write an autumn poem
I want to write an autumn poem
I want to write an autumn poem

I want to write an autumn poem
I want to write an autumn poem
I want to write an autumn poem
I want to write an autumn poem

I want to write an autumn poem
I want to write an autumn poem
I want to write an autumn poem
I want to write an autumn poem

I want to write an autumn poem
I want to write an autumn poem
I want to write an autumn poem
I want to write an autumn poem

insanity

I want to write a poem about insanity
sometimes so close to me
I want to write a poem about insanity
sometimes so close to me

I want to write a poem about insanity
sometimes so close to me
I want to write a poem about insanity
sometimes so close to me

I want to write a poem about insanity
sometimes so close to me
I want to write a poem about insanity
sometimes so close to me

I want to write a poem about insanity
sometimes so close to me
I want to write a poem about insanity
sometimes so close to me

poem

I want to write a poem in which every line is different
I want to write a poem in which every line is different
I want to write a poem in which every line is different
I want to write a poem in which every line is different

I want to write a poem in which every line is different
I want to write a poem in which every line is different
I want to write a poem in which every line is different
I want to write a poem in which every line is different

I want to write a poem in which every line is different
I want to write a poem in which every line is different
I want to write a poem in which every line is different
I want to write a poem in which every line is different

I want to write a poem in which every line is different
I want to write a poem in which every line is different
I want to write a poem in which every line is different
I want to write a poem in which every line is different

new poem

I want to write a poem that does not yet exist
I want to write a poem that does not yet exist
I want to write a poem that does not yet exist
I want to write a poem that does not yet exist

I want to write a poem that does not yet exist
I want to write a poem that does not yet exist
I want to write a poem that does not yet exist
I want to write a poem that does not yet exist

I want to write a poem that does not yet exist
I want to write a poem that does not yet exist
I want to write a poem that does not yet exist
I want to write a poem that does not yet exist

I want to write a poem that does not yet exist
I want to write a poem that does not yet exist
I want to write a poem that does not yet exist
I want to write a poem that does not yet exist

i make a new poem out of old poems

the ship has a leak
the heart full of wounds
the crane is drawn to the rushes
blood oranges roll toward black seas
the tree defiantly raises its arm
nobody loves me
on the steps of melancholy
the rock is blind
nothing for it
we don't play the dances anymore

poem (for marxists)

I still have to go to the bank
class struggle is intensifying
maybe I'll stop by this evening
class struggle is intensifying
I'll call you wednesday or thursday
class struggle is intensifying
I'll write you
class struggle is intensifying
I'll be back again in a week
class struggle is intensifying
alright then
class struggle is intensifying

poem (for nature lovers)

I still have to go to the bank
the may sun shines warm
maybe I'll stop by this evening
the may sun shines warm
I'll call you wednesday or thursday
the may sun shines warm
I'll write you
the may sun shines warm
I'll be back again in a week
the may sun shines warm
alright then
the may sun shines warm

poem (for the suicidal) 1

I still have to go to the bank
it can't go on like this
maybe I'll stop by this evening
it can't go on like this
I'll call you wednesday or thursday
it can't go on like this
I'll write you
it can't go on like this
I'll be back again in a week
it can't go on like this
alright then
it can't go on like this

poem (for the suicidal) 2

I still have to go to the bank
there's always a way out
maybe I'll stop by this evening
there's always a way out
I'll call you wednesday or thursday
there's always a way out
I'll write you
there's always a way out
I'll be back again in a week
there's always a way out
alright then
there's always a way out

Novels About Novels

Taken From Life

The trainer had green eyes. The trainer went into the cage and was torn apart by the lions. Lions are carnivores. Lions feed on zebras and antelope. Zebras and antelope feed on grass. Grass is green. Green is the color of hope. Hopefully nothing will happen. Nothing's going to happen, thought the trainer with the green eyes, as she went into the lions' cage.

Rainer's Novel

Born in Vienna. School in Vienna. Foreign Legion in North Africa. Banking apprenticeship in Vienna. Marriage in Vienna. Divorce in Vienna. Second marriage in Vienna. Birth of a daughter. Divorce in Vienna. Short stays in Munich. Lives in Vienna.

Happy Ending

The express train passes through Hütteldorf-Hacking station. Gerngross department store is on Mariahilfer Strasse. The Thirteen crosses the Wien River. The old woman gets off. The gust of wind rattles the gate. Inside the house it's dark and gloomy. The big room is dusty. The round table is in the middle. In the matchbox there are three thumbtacks.

Family Chronicle

The back room is in the back. The children's room is next to it. The living room is in the front. The bedroom is in between. In the kitchen there is a light on. The silverware is in the drawer on the right. The plates are at the top of the sideboard. The pots and pans are at the bottom of the sideboard. Dinner is ready. The TV is on. The program ends. The child goes into the children's room. The TV is turned off. The parents go into the bedroom. The light is turned off.

?

their coloration varies from white to pink and violet to
blackish-brown
some are long and thin others short and pudgy
their texture is inconsistent
some have a fortified upper end
they contain a fluid
under certain conditions they harden
they can be used in a number of ways
they are different in china
in certain species of birds they are particularly large
they play an important role in reproduction
their primary component is protein
no two are alike

credo

each day god supplies us with bulgarian tomatoes *connective element* i use the german language and am committed to anarchism *connective element* this is my pledge to anarchism *connective element* tichy's ice cream dumplings—a dream *connective element* female seeking male *connective element* male seeking female *connective element* vienna offers many possibilities *connective element* amorous couples keep inventing new *connective element* children drown in rivers are run over by cars fall out of windows *connective element* as the saying goes, when it rains it pours *connective element* what heat *connective element* now men and women can swim in the old branch of the danube drink beer in the prater and take two sleeping pills before bed *connective element* true

The Spoon as Hero

Photos: full face
              in profile
              while eating

1. the spoon is bought: date and location of purchase
2. delivery company and/or manufacturer of spoon
3. nature and production of spoon:
     a) what material is the spoon made from
     b) where does it come from
     c) treatment of the material, work method
     d) how many workers are involved
     e) how many spoons are produced per unit of time
     f) where are they delivered
4. use of the spoon:
     a) eating soups, vegetables, porridges, preserves, taking medicine
     b) manner of eating
5. etymology of the word "spoon"
6. quotes about "spoon": various

this and that

and stairs and house walls
and house walls and brick walls and walls and walls
and brick walls and windows
and cars
and old women and daring
and cars and television sets and wireless radios
and tape recorders and special offers
and trams
and saleswomen and rye bread and wachauer rolls
and dark bread and apple strudel
and saleswomen and pork chops and drumsticks
and pork knuckles and children and cigarettes and newspapers
and old women and women and men and trucks
and skirts and blouses and sweaters and suits
and spinach and oranges and cucumbers and radishes
and saleswomen and sugar and rum and margarine
and grape juice and lemons and white rolls and eggs
and liquor and women and sausage and preserves
and toilet paper and ballpoint pens and women and women
and children and men
and cars

Peter does everything I say

Peter does only what I say that Peter does

I say, Peter learned to read, write and do arithmetic properly. Peter goes to work every day. Peter has a new car. Peter has a wife and one daughter. Peter earns a good living and saves part of his earnings. On Saturdays Peter washes his car. On Sundays he drives out to the country with his wife and daughter. Peter likes to eat schnitzel, liver dumpling soup, pork knuckles, apple strudel, Liptauer cheese. Peter likes everything to be in its place. When something is lying around, he puts it away. Last Sunday it rained and Peter couldn't leave the house. After breakfast he smoked three cigarettes, took a bath and shaved. Then he went for a short walk and brought back sweets and the newspaper. Peter enjoyed lunch that day. He drank several glasses of red wine. After lunch Peter read the newspaper and fell asleep. In the evening he asked his wife, "How about a movie?" Peter went to a movie with his wife. The movie was interesting. After the movie Peter wanted to have a beer, but his wife had a headache from the air in the movie theater. So Peter walked home with his wife. Peter turned on the light and sank into an armchair. He took off his shoes and drank a cognac. His wife was already in bed. Peter lay down next to her and touched her on the shoulder. The woman smiled amiably. Peter turned over and thought about the movie, the apartment of a family they knew and the upcoming summer vacation. Peter smoked another cigarette and opened the window. If you go to bed early, you're fresh in the morning, Peter thought, I say.

This is how the novel begins:

The left hand reaches for the clock, it is 7:30 a.m. The blanket is thrown back, the yellow-orange wool socks are pulled on, the gray cloth shoes over them. The window is opened. The red cardigan is put on over the long red nightgown. On the first floor, the light is switched on. The plug of the electric hotplate is inserted into the socket. The door to the street is opened. The toilet is used, water flows into the yellow plastic basin, the faucet is turned off, water is poured into the toilet. The hair is touched with both hands. The pot with the black handle is half-filled with water and set on the electric hotplate. Two mugs are set on the table and small spoons are laid next to them. Tea is transferred from the tea packet labeled "India Special" into one of the mugs with one small spoon, coffee is transferred from the jar of instant coffee into the other mug with the other spoon. A wooden board is set between the two mugs. The butter is laid on the wooden board, the butter's silver paper wrapping is opened. The cheese, taken out from two layers of paper, goes next to the butter. The paper is set on a stool. The mortadella, wrapped in paper, goes on the wooden board next to the cheese. Three thick slices of white bread are cut with the large knife and put on a plate. One plate and one knife go next to each mug, one knife with a yellow horn handle, the second with a wooden handle. Both mugs, the one with tea and the one with coffee, are filled with boiling water. The pot with the boiling water is set on the hotplate, two eggs are lowered into the boiling water. A spoonful of sugar is put into the mug of coffee, a slice of white bread is smeared with butter, a piece of cheese is cut. Some coffee is drunk, some bread and cheese is eaten. The eggs are removed from the boiling water with a tablespoon. Each egg is held briefly under cold running water. The eggs are placed on the table in egg cups. Part of the shell is removed, salt from the salt cellar is sprinkled on the egg. The eggs are eaten with small spoons. The bread and cheese is eaten up, the coffee is drunk up, the tea is drunk up. Two spoonfuls of coffee from the jar of instant coffee are put into the coffee mug, the pot with the black handle is taken off of the hotplate, the mug is filled with boiling water. The tea mug is refilled with boiling water. A cigarette is lit. Coffee is drunk from the coffee mug, tea is drunk from the tea mug. The cigarette is stubbed out, the plates are cleared of crumbs, cheese rinds and eggshells. All the trash is emptied onto one plate and thrown into the trash bin. The plates are stacked on top of each other on the bench next to the table. The mugs are placed next to them. The toilet is used, water flows into the yellow plastic basin, the faucet is turned off, water is poured into the toilet. The pot with the black handle is filled with water, the pot is placed on the hotplate. On the top floor, the blankets are taken off the bed one by one, shaken out and laid on top of the red bench. The sheet is smoothed out. The top sheet is spread over the bed. The gray checkered blanket is spread over the left half of the bed. The two colorful checkered car blankets are spread over the right half of the bed. The gray blanket with the holes and white spots is spread over the bed. The top sheet is folded back over the blankets. The hand towel, the underwear, the sweater, the pants are taken down from the line and carried to the ground floor. The front door is closed. The pot is taken off the hotplate and the hot water is emptied into the yellow plastic basin. The pot is filled with cold water and placed on the hotplate. Cold water is let into the yellow plastic basin until the water in the basin is lukewarm. The nightgown is taken off. Face and neck are washed. The teeth are brushed. Face, neck and hands are dried off, the underwear is put on. The pants and the sweater are put on. The comb is taken out of the bag on the bench next to the table. The hair is combed. The shoelaces are tied. Nightgown and hand towel are hung on the line on the top floor. The watch is put on. The ashtray is emptied. A lemon is sliced in two and pressed into a cup. Cold water is added. The lemonade is drunk. A cigarette is lit. A book is picked up and opened. The cigarette is smoked. The front door is opened. The book is closed and laid down. The light on the ground floor is switched off. The front door is closed.

I

I am a good person
this is true
I am a cold person
this is true
I am a sensitive person
this is true
I am an untidy person
this is true
I am an open person
this is true

I'm either tired or rested
I'm either hungry or full
I'm either sober or drunk
I'm either dirty or clean
I'm either dressed or naked
I'm either excited or calm

I have a homeland no I don't
I have a car I no I don't
I have two hands no I don't
I have good luck no I don't
I have a child no I don't

someday I'd like to be rosy
someday I'd like to laugh
someday I'd like to be twenty
and dive in with a splash

I will never sink in the sea
and never scream with a toothache
I'll never drown in sour milk
and never be in zurich

always I will be radiant
always full of joy
always I'll be obedient
always not just today

why — because

I'm dying because I have cancer
I'm dying because everyone dies
I'm dying because I'm old
I'm dying because there's a war
I'm dying because a car has run over me

I'm eating because I'm hungry
I'm eating because it's time to eat
I'm eating because I like the taste
I'm eating because nourishment is necessary

I'm talking because I want to say something
I'm talking because I have a tongue
I'm talking because I'm happy
I'm talking because I'm sad
I'm talking because I don't want to be impolite

I'm reading because I'm bored
I'm reading because I'm interested in something
I'm reading because I want to be informed
I'm reading because I can't sleep

I'm sleeping because I'm tired
I'm sleeping because the body needs sleep
I'm sleeping because it's night
I'm sleeping because otherwise I'll be tired tomorrow

I'm drinking because everyone is drinking
I'm drinking because the wine is so good
I'm drinking because I'm thirsty
I'm drinking because it makes me funny
I'm drinking because I want to get drunk

someday I'd like to be hard as steel
someday I'd like to make goulash
someday I'd like to delight you all
and dive in with a splash

I'll never suffer in the dark
and never guard the goal
I'll never avoid a national park
and never be in zurich

always I will be expensive
always have my sorrows
always I'll be lathered up
always not just tomorrow

"How are you?"

i'm good
i'm really good
i'm just fine
i'm doing great
i'm not doing so well
i'm alright, really
i've never been better
i'm fine, actually
i'm actually just fine
i'm not really doing too well
i'm really great
i'm really not doing so well
i'm actually just great
i'm actually not doing so well
i've really never been better
i'm really doing great
i'm really doing well
i'm really doing pretty well
i'm really good, actually
i'm actually really great
i'm actually really just fine
i'm actually not doing all that well
i've actually never been better
i'm really doing just great
i'm actually really not doing well
i'm actually really not doing so well
i'm actually doing just fine, really

someday I'd like to be flammable
someday I'd like to burn like trash
someday I'd like to be a boxer
and dive in with a splash

I will never run in dreams
nor ever borrow wings
I'll never drown in the river inn
and never be in zurich

always I'll be ignitable
and always get my pay
always I will be forthright
always not just today

Important!

Rainer Pichler always says the same thing.
 "I have everything with me."

Bodo Hell always says the same thing.
 "The phone just keeps ringing."

Uta Prantl always says the same thing.
 "We'll be away over the weekend."

Walter Ramstorfer always says the same thing.
 "Let's talk about it next time."

Günter Leikauf always says the same thing.
 "I won't be staying long."

Hannes Schneider always says the same thing.
 "The whole thing should just be blown up."

Bernt Burchhart always says the same thing.
 "There's poetry in your blood."

Elfriede Gerstl always says the same thing.
 "I really need to find an apartment."

Gerwart Brandl always says the same thing.
 "I'm busy Tuesday nights."

Liesl Ujvary always says the same thing.
 "I still have work to do."

someday I'd like to be ice-cold
someday ignite a blaze
someday I'd like to find true faith
and dive in with a splash

I will never die in bed
never forget the pledge
I will never rot in vienna
and never be in zurich

I will always be delicious
full of people here to stay
I will always do the dishes
always not just today

what I write

I write everything that I write
I see everything that I see
I hear everything that I hear
I read everything that I read
I drink everything that I drink
I eat everything that I eat
I sing everything that I sing
I say everything that I say
I earn everything that I earn
I hate everything that I hate
I love everything that I love
I have everything that I have
I dream everything that I dream
I do everything that I do

someday I'd like to be left behind
and laugh at all the world
someday I'd like to shine with dew
and dive in headlong

I will never build a house
nor be a dirty swine
I'll never want to do without you
and never be in zurich

always I'll be eating ducks
and howling with the fray
always I will forget fritz
always not just today

Food

For breakfast, coffee.
Real instant bean coffee, four small spoons per cup, two tablets of sweetener, some milk. Two cups.
If plenty was eaten the day before, just coffee.
If little was eaten, bread and butter as well.
Rye bread with margarine.
After three to four hours, a feeling of hunger.
Lemonade made from two lemons and cold water, no sugar.
After a while, increasing hunger.
For lunch, soup, a ready-made flour-based soup, mushy, not much flavor. Bread on the side, a bit of cheese.
For lunch, nothing fried, nothing spicy, no seasoning, no fat.
Often, desire for meat.
After meat, great exhaustion.
Later tea, strong, several cups.
A piece of bread, a can of liver paté.
On some days, wine.
If wine, hunger.
Desire for meat, spice, seasoning. Onions, mustard, horseradish, pepper.
Desire for more wine.
Later an aspirin, some water, sometimes with lemon.
Always craving for fat.
Often, desire for fatty meat. Kaiserfleisch, roast pork, pork knuckle, goose, bacon.
Sometimes a strong desire for sweets. Chocolate with nuts.
Often, thirst. Water, tea, lemonade.
Regular, nourishing, plentiful food.

At Home

Wake up. Breakfast at eight.
Two cups of weak coffee with milk. A cigarette.
Radio: Studio Tyrol, today's weather.
Question: What's for lunch today?
Tidy up, make beds, get dressed.
A walk. Question: Where are you going?
The Achenweg down to the bypass ring road, the Hornweg, up the Lower Gänsbachgasse, the Pfarrauweg, the Lebenbergweg over the Lebenberg to Bichlach. Beware of dogs! The Lebenbergweg back, down by the Lauchenbauer house, Josef Pirchl Strasse, along Bahnhofstrasse and back to Klausnerfeld.
Question: Where were you? Did you meet anyone?
Set the table. Plates, spoons, forks, knives. Glasses. Red wine, mineral water. Napkins.
Lunch.
Radio: Traffic bulletin. The news.
Red wine and a cigarette.
Dry the dishes.
A crime novel, an hour's nap.
Tea time. A cup of coffee with milk, a cigarette.
Two hours or so of work at the desk.
A walk. Question: Now?
Over the train tracks, up the Ölberg to the Tennerhof, the Römerweg, down to Felseneck, take Achenweg back to Klausnerfeld.
Supper. Red wine.
TV, *Österreichbild*, ads, the week to come, *Zeit im Bild*.
Red wine, a cigarette. Ads, sports, ads.
Turn off the TV.
Two hours or so of work at the desk.
Finish the crime novel.

A banana. A cigarette.
Sleep.

Sleep

Wait until you feel tired.
When tiredness arrives, ignore it at first.
When tiredness returns, gradually bring work to a close.
Open windows, place a chair beside the bed, pull back the covers. Smoke a cigarette in the hallway in front of the mirror. Close windows, lower shades, remove watch and place beside the bed. Get a glass of water from the kitchen and set beside the bed. Empty the ashtray and set beside the bed. Place cigarettes and lighter beside it. A book. Take off clothes. Hang trousers over the hook, sweater over the chair, set shoes in the corner. Put on slippers. Wash with warm water in the bathroom. Dry off. Put on night dress.
Lie down in bed, read a few pages, smoke a cigarette, wait for tiredness to intensify.
Turn off light, lie awake on your back with your head propped up.
Upon waking, check the clock to see if sleep was sufficient.

Autobiography with Instructions

1. A Bit About Myself

My name is Liesl Ujvary. I am 36 years old. I was born in Pressburg and have lived in Vienna for three years. I've been interested in foreign languages and far-away countries since I was a child. I attended grammar school and then studied Slavic languages at the University of Vienna. I began teaching while still at university. At 21, I got married. My husband was a land surveyor. We got divorced three years later. I have a twelve-year-old daughter. Her name is Hanna. Hanna lives in Tyrol with my parents. Now I work in the field of literature. I compose stories and poems dealing with various questions of our time. I'm interested in art, theater, music, sports and anything new. I often go to exhibits or to the movies. My hobby is hiking. On the weekends, I go on outings in the countryside around Vienna alone or with friends. Once a month, I visit my parents.

Please answer the following questions:
1. What is your name?
2. Where do you live?
3. Where were you born?
4. How old are you?
5. Are you married?
6. Do you have children?
7. What is your son's (your daughter's) name?
8. What is your profession?
9. Where did you go to school?
10. Do you love your work?
11. Do you love music?
12. What do you do in your free time?
13. Do you go to the theater often?

2. My Family

This is my father. His name is Robert Maier. He is 75 years old. My mother's name is Maria Maier. She is 69 years old. When they were young, my parents lived in Pressburg, where they met each other and got married. Later, they moved to a little town in Tyrol. My father owned a hair salon where he and my mother worked. Now they no longer work. They're retired. My parents have two children—me and my brother. My brother is named Robert, just like my father. He is four years younger than I am. Robert looks like my mother. He has reddish hair, blue eyes and freckles. Robert is a psychologist. He is interested in cognitive development in children. Robert is a cheerful, lively, sharply focused man. He has many friends. The atmosphere in our family is very friendly. We write frequently and visit each other whenever possible.

Please answer the following questions:
1. Where do your parents live?
2. What is your father's name?
3. How old is he?
4. What is your mother's name?
5. How old is she?
6. What is your father's profession?
7. Do your parents still work?
8. Do you have siblings?
9. What is your brother's (your sister's) job?
10. What is the atmosphere like in your family?
11. Do you keep in touch with your family members?

3. My Building and My Apartment

As I already said, I live in Vienna. I have an apartment not far from the city center, in Vienna's 4th district. The building I live in is on a busy street. It was built in 1960 and has eight floors. My apartment is on the 8th floor. It has two rooms: a living room and a bedroom. The doorways of both rooms lead into a narrow hallway that is 6 meters long. Between the bedroom and the living room are the kitchen and the bathroom. Across from the bathroom is the separate WC. The apartment is quite cozy, warm, light and comfortable. The windows in the living room face southeast, in the other rooms they face northeast. The living room is the largest room in the apartment. In the middle of this room are a round table and a few chairs. To the right of the door is a tile stove; to the left of the door is a couch. On the opposite wall, there are shelves with books. In the corner by the window there is a desk. There is a large rug on the floor. Across from the door is a large window and the door to the balcony. Flowers bloom on the balcony all summer long.

Please answer the following questions:
1. Where do you live?
2. How many floors does your building have?
3. Which floor is your apartment on?
4. How many rooms does your apartment have?
5. What furniture do you have in your living room?
6. What furniture do you have in your bedroom?
7. Which direction do the windows in your apartment face?
8. Is there a full bath in your apartment?
9. Does your apartment have central heating?
10. Where is your desk?
11. Where is your TV?
12. Where is your bookcase?

4. My Day

I am a writer and work from home. I don't always wake up at the same time. Sometimes I get up a bit earlier, sometimes a bit later. After getting up, I drink two cups of coffee and skim through my papers while smoking a cigarette. Then I make the bed and do some housekeeping. I do morning exercises every day, then shower. Before noon, I go out to pick up the newspaper and buy something for lunch. After lunch I relax a bit, read or think about things, sometimes I make notes, and now and again I sit down at the typewriter. In the evening, I go to a café or to a show or visit friends. We exchange news and talk about all kinds of problems. This sometimes continues until very late. Before going to sleep, I usually read a few more pages of a book.

Please answer the following questions:
1. Where do you work?
2. What is your profession?
3. Where is your factory, institute, bank located?
4. When do you wake up?
5. Do you do morning exercises?
6. What do you eat for breakfast?
7. When do you leave the house?
8. Do you walk to work or do you drive?
9. When do you begin working?
10. Where and when do you usually eat lunch?
11. When do you stop working?
12. When do you come home?
13. What do you do in the evening?
14. When do you go to sleep?

5. Errands

When I have errands to run in the city, I take the tram. The tram stop is just two minutes away from my building. I always get on the conductorless car. I ride four stops to the opera. Then I continue on foot. There is no public transportation in Vienna's city center, the Innere Stadt (that's the name of the district). Soon it will be possible to reach the center of Vienna quickly and easily with the U-Bahn, which is under construction. At Karlsplatz I take the Stadtbahn six stops to Friedensbrücke. The Stadtbahn runs partly underground, partly as an elevated line. It's a comfortable and quick mode of transport. On the Stadtbahn and the tram, passengers' tickets are sometimes checked by ticket inspectors. The ticket inspectors wear dark gray uniforms. At Friedensbrücke, I get on tram number 5 and take it a few stops to Alser Strasse, where bus line 13 A ends. The Thirteen, as people call this line, is a large double-decker bus that runs on liquid petroleum gas. I take the Thirteen straight through the other districts, to the stop just in front of my building. The trip takes about twenty minutes, a bit longer in heavy traffic.

Please answer the following questions:
1. What mode of transportation do you use to get into the city?
2. Does public transportation run on your street?
3. How many stops does it take to reach the city center?
4. Do you have to change trains, perhaps even several times?
5. Do you use the conductorless car?
6. Does your city have an underground rail system?
7. Do you buy a ticket in advance and validate it at a machine upon boarding?
8. Have you ever been caught by a ticket inspector without a valid ticket?
9. Have you ever been on a double-decker bus?
10. How long does it take from the city center to your building?

6. An Outing to the Countryside

I love nature. On Sundays, when the weather is nice, I like to go on outings to the countryside. I usually make plans with a friend, and we drive a car, take the train or ride our bikes out of the city. We're both enthusiastic cyclists, so we often ride our bikes. First we ride through the city until we reach the Danube, following all the traffic rules. Once we've reached the Danube, we decide whether to go upriver or downriver. Downriver, for a long time the path along the Danube leads past the factories and tanks of the oil refinery, into the Lobau nature reserve. When we go there, we swim in the abandoned canal that was once to connect the rivers Danube and Oder and hike in the littoral woodlands. On the way home, we stop at a rural winery for a glass of wine. When we cycle upriver, we pass by meadows and garden plots and after a while reach the foot of the Bisamberg. A well-known wine-making area surrounds the Bisamberg. On the way around Bisamberg, we stop at several rural wineries and simple restaurants. We get home late in the evening, tired and happy.

Please answer the following questions:
1. Do you love nature?
2. Where do you usually spend your Sundays?
3. Do you go into nature?
4. Where do you usually go on Sundays?
5. Do you travel by car or by train?
6. Can you ride a bike?
7. Do you like to hike?
8. Where do you have a picnic?
9. Can you swim?
10. Do you often stop at wineries or restaurants?
11. When do you get home?
12. Do you often go on outings to the countryside?

7. Visiting a Friend

My friend's name is Linde. Linde is 35 years old. She is married, her husband's name is Istvan. Istvan is an ear, nose and throat doctor. Linde has a son, Philipp. Philipp is a year and a half old, he can't speak yet. First, Linde puts Philipp to bed. Sometimes Philipp cries for a little bit. Then we prepare dinner. Linde puts bacon, sausage, cheese, hard-boiled eggs, butter, bread and tomatoes on a plate, I set the table. Before dinner we have an aperitif, and with dinner we drink a bottle of red or white wine. We talk while we eat. Linde tells me about Philipp, I tell her about my daughter, Hanna. Linde has a hard time finding a babysitter. We also talk about mutual friends and about our health. Linde tells me that she had a cold. I smoke a few cigarettes after dinner, then the table is cleared. We continue discussing news about cultural life. Linde is a cheerful person, there's always something to laugh about with her. Istvan comes home later and drives me home in his car.

Please answer the following questions:
1. Do you have many friends?
2. What is your friend's name?
3. Are they married?
4. Do you know any married couples with children?
5. Are you often invited to dinner?
6. What do you drink with dinner?
7. Do you prefer red or white wine?
8. What do you talk about?
9. Do you like to talk about your health?
10. Do you talk about mutual acquaintances?
11. Is your friend interested in the arts?
12. When do you go home?

8. Sick

Overexertion often leads to illness. My throat hurts, my joints ache, I shiver, I feel cold. I pick up the thermometer and take my temperature: 38.3°C! I have tonsillitis. I make myself hot tea, take an aspirin and get in bed. I sweat. I feel a little better the next morning. I'm not able to get up yet. I stay in bed and sleep a lot. A friend calls and asks if she should bring me anything, but there is nothing I need. I have no appetite. I have a fever again in the evening. On the third day, I'm still too weak to get up. My throat hurts when I swallow. I worry. I check my medicine cabinet and see that I have an antibiotic. I take the antibiotic in the prescribed dosage. The next day, I'm pain-free and my temperature is normal. I'm still weak, my complexion is pale. I have to take it easy for the next few days until I'm completely healthy.

Please answer the following questions:
1. When were you last ill?
2. Did you catch a cold?
3. Do you suffer from headaches?
4. Do you frequently have a high fever?
5. Do you know a doctor?
6. Who takes care of you when you get sick?
7. Do you believe that sweating is healthy?
8. Do you have poor circulation?
9. Is your blood pressure too high or too low?
10. Do you take antibiotics?
11. Have you ever had surgery?
12. Are you overweight?
13. Do you have heart problems?

9. At the Supermarket

When I need something, I go to the supermarket. Our supermarket has everything: fruit and vegetables, dairy products, imported goods, bread, sweets, alcohol, cheese and sausage, meat, canned goods, household items, soaps and laundry detergent, cosmetics. There are small carts by the entrance, which make shopping easy and comfortable. First I choose 1 kilo of sugar cubes and a small packet of Splendor Italian rice. Canned stuffed pepper is on special today: 13.90 instead of 16.90. In the fruit and vegetable section, I buy 1 kilo of apples of the "Kronprinz" variety and 10 lemons. Here, a saleswoman assists the customers, who mustn't touch the produce. In the bread department, I buy a 1-kilo loaf of dark bread and a slice of apple strudel. Now I'm at the wine section. The selection is large. I deliberate and decide on a bottle of Tunisian red. In the sausage section, I buy 10 decagrams of Heurigen salami and decagrams of Austrian Tilsiter cheese. There's nothing else I need. I push my cart to the register and wait until it's my turn. I put my shopping on the conveyor belt and the cashier rings the prices up at the register. 64.70 all together. I pay, pack up my purchases, and leave the store.

Please answer the following questions:
1. Do you enjoy grocery shopping?
2. Is there a supermarket in your neighborhood?
3. What are the advantages of self-service?
4. How much does a kilo of sugar cost?
5. Do you buy bread at a bakery or at the supermarket?
6. Do you go grocery shopping often?
7. How much does a liter of milk cost?
8. On which days do you do a lot of shopping?
9. Do you look for discounts?
10. Do you like to try out new products?
11. Do you prefer fresh dishes to canned foods?
12. Do you favor domestic over foreign products?
13. Does your supermarket also carry sewing needles?

10. A Party

We're having a party today. Everything is ready: vodka, whiskey, beer, a couple bottles of fruit schnaps, some double-liters of red and white wine. That will be enough. We'll have cold meats and cheeses to eat, sprats, herring, head cheese in vinegar and oil, pickles, tomatoes, rolls, salted breadsticks, dark rye, white bread. There's also a big pot of Szegedin goulash. The table needs to be set: I carry wine glasses, beer mugs, and schnaps glasses into the living room, set the plates on the table, lay out the silverware, fetch paper napkins and lay out the cold dishes. Everyone can help themselves to as much as they like. We still need a corkscrew and bottle opener. The ashtrays need to be emptied and washed. Now everything is ready. The doorbell rings. Bernt and Petra are at the door. We're eager for the party to begin. Soon the other guests come. Heidi and Rainer, Günter, Helmut and Christa, Rita and Hans, Karl and Uta, Walter Ramstorfer, Meina Schellander, Bodo Hell, Linde and Istvan, Hasso, Wolfgang, Kurt, Viktoria and Maria Hromatka. The first bottles are opened, everyone raises their glasses and toasts. Kurt tells a story about a car accident. Everyone laughs. It will be an entertaining evening.

Please answer the following questions:
1. Do you love parties?
2. Are you alone a lot?
3. Do you have friends?
4. Do you like to drink alcoholic drinks?
5. What is your favorite drink?
6. Do you like to drink schnaps with beer?
7. How do you set the table?
8. Which appetizers do you recommend for a party?
9. Do you have enough glasses?
10. When do the first guests arrive?
11. What is the most important thing for a good party?

12. How long does a real party last?
13. Are there sometimes leftovers after a party?

11. Visiting My Parents

My parents live in Kitzbühel, a small town in Tyrol. There's a good train from Vienna to Kitzbühel, the Arlberg Express. The journey takes six and a half hours. My daughter and my father usually pick me up from the train. We exchange greetings, excited to see each other. The house my parents live in is in Klausnerfeld, very close to the train station. At home, I see my mother. I get a good meal that my mother has prepared for me. I ask Hanna and my parents how they're doing and what's new with them. Hanna tells me about school and about her friends. My parents ask about my work and the weather in Vienna. Afterwards, I go for a walk. I go for walks often in Kitzbühel—up the Ölberg, along Römerweg to Vordergrub and back along the river, or up over the Lebenberg to the Schwarzsee, or else along the Sonnberg toward Hagstein. I know every house and every tree out there. I enjoy these walks very much, since I feel very good when I'm in nature. In the evenings I drink a glass of wine with my parents while we see what's on TV. After nine, we all go to sleep. I always feel rejuvenated back home, the quiet life, good food and fresh mountain air do me good. I usually stay three or four days, then go back to Vienna.

Please answer the following questions:
1. Where do your parents live?
2. Do you visit your parents frequently?
3. Is your mother a good cook?
4. How do you feel when you're with your parents?
5. Do your parents live in the country/in the mountains?
6. Do you go for many walks in your parents' area?
7. Do you watch TV with your parents in the evening?
8. When do your parents go to sleep?
9. Are you able to rest and rejuvenate back home?
10. Do your parents lead a quiet life?
11. How long do you usually stay with your parents?

12. My Daughter

My daughter's name is Hanna. Hanna turned 12 last June. She has dark blond hair and brown eyes, she's strong, very agile and a good athlete. Hanna is now in her third year of secondary school. She is a diligent, ambitious child and gets on well at school, even if she has difficulties in some subjects, like math and English. Hanna likes to be around other children, the company of adults bores her. She's interested in sports and geography. When sports are on TV, Hanna always watches, especially when it's skiing. She's a very good skier herself. She goes ice skating in late fall, swimming and cycling in the summer. Hanna grows more confident and independent with each passing year. When she comes to Vienna, she takes the train by herself. She doesn't like to leave home, though, and gets homesick easily. Hanna has a lot of friends among the children in Klausnerfeld and likes spending time in the courtyard where all the kids play. That's where she feels most herself. She always looks forward to school holidays. She wants a radio for Christmas.

Please answer the following questions:
1. Do you have children?
2. Do you like children?
3. How old is your son/your daughter?
4. What color are your child's hair and eyes?
5. Does your child go to school yet?
6. Does your child like going to school?
7. Does your child have difficulties in school?
8. What is your child interested in?
9. Is your child sturdy or scrawny?
10. Does your child do sports?
11. Is your child timid?
12. Does your child like to play with other children or do they prefer to be alone?
13. What does your child want for Christmas?

Out with It!

The Body

My body is weak, substantially weakened by the irregularities that constitute my life. One irregularity follows another, everything or almost everything I do, what I eat, what I drink, how I work, how I sleep, all of it is unnatural and continually harms my body. No wonder my body breaks down every couple weeks, or rather every few days, refusing its services and seeking refuge in some ostensible illness, such as endless colds, backaches, kidney ailments, to name just a few of these illnesses, whose medical reality does undeniably exist and which are indeed regularly resolved by the appropriate treatments and medications, but are nonetheless ostensible illnesses, not caused by unlucky accidents and the random circulation of viruses or bacteria, but rather nothing less than the logical consequences of my irregular, unnatural way of living, which incidentally is not mine alone, but likewise constitutes the lifestyle of nearly all modern people, for which reason nearly all people suffer, just like me, from their sickened, weakened bodies.

Out with It!

My Profession

My profession guarantees no stable income, no job security, no health insurance, no pension in old age. Society values my profession very little. Newspapers and magazines, radio and television, the media with which my profession should have a close and direct relationship, are hardly interested in my contributions. When I apply to them, I'm dismissed or fended off with offers of badly paid, subordinate jobs. If I want to begin a project about an area outside the scope of my own life, I receive neither material nor organizational support from anyone. So I have no way to make my work useful to society. I can do nothing but describe how useful work is prevented. If I try to portray or promote any other way of living beyond the conventionally established options for human existence, my efforts are ignored, ridiculed or labeled delusional. All my colleagues find themselves in the same situation.

Out with It!

The Apartment

My apartment is too hot in summer, the sun burns down on the flat roof and the windows, in winter it's cold and drafty due to the many exterior walls, frequent stormy winds rattle the windows and doors, howl through the chimneys and flues. Like the rest of the building, my apartment is an example of architectural mindlessness and shoddy execution of details. The rooms are narrow and badly layed out, the walls don't keep out any noise, the windows are far too large and set in inappropriate places, the heating problem remains unsolved, or is expensive. The kitchen can't be heated at all, it's cold underfoot due to the stone floor, making the room unusable as a living space in the colder months. The bathroom and toilet are windowless closets. The apartment's biggest and most serious flaw, however, is its location on a heavily trafficked intersection. In summer, you can't have a conversation or work with the windows open. The street noise makes all thought impossible, not to mention the insomnia. The apartment is relatively cheap and centrally located, unfortunately it doesn't allow for a normal life.

Out with It!

The Family

There's always trouble with my family. The reason for these difficulties is that my family, specifically my parents, don't accept my lifestyle. My way of life seems suspect to them because it doesn't seem to lead to external success in the bourgeois sense. If you don't make a lot of money, you amount to nothing, my parents think. My parents would like to see me with a secure job or married to a husband who has a good, safe job, building an existence for myself, as they put it. My views on life and my work are incomprehensible to them, they can't imagine how someone could live, or would want to live, this way. This lack of understanding is expressed through ongoing dissatisfaction with countless small details regarding my lifestyle. My parents criticize my clothing, my hairstyle, my handbag, my choice of friends, my eating and sleeping habits, my political views, that I smoke too much and so forth. Whenever I try to have a conversation with my parents and justify my way of life, I come up against incomprehension and refusal.

"Sealed Object with List of Contents"

A small wooden box, each side measuring 50 cm, beech, slightly grainy, a door on the front, it is locked, the key inserted. Inside the box is the list of contents.

List of Contents

1. Sealed Object
2. List of Contents
3. letters A–Z
4. natural numbers
5. other numbers
6. German
7. other languages
8. words
9. grammar
10. I
11. you
12. he
13. she
14. it
15. we
16. you (pl.)
17. they
18. the world
19. objects
20. soldiers
21. dogs
22. Vienna
23. the blue sky
24. porn magazines
25. coffeehouses
26. love

27. emigrants
28. new emigrants
29. friends
30. enemies
31. the opposite
32. depression
33. leftists
34. rightists
35. Marxists
36. the universe
37. sunflowers
38. other flowers
39. schnaps
40. the Autobahn
41. Coca-Cola
42. Pepsi-Cola
43. hospitals
44. cops
45. primary schools
46. railways
47. one-way streets
48. trams
49. people from Linz
50. people from Graz
51. the Swiss
52. other nationalities
53. the Jews
54. the Russians
55. antisemites
56. anticommunists
57. teachers
58. archaeologists
59. psychologists
60. homosexuals

61. painters
62. everything
63. keys
64. locks
65. clocks
66. magazines
67. books
68. schoolbooks
69. supermarkets
70. work
71. free time
72. money
73. mistakes
74. order
75. laws
76. children
77. medicine
78. beds
79. hell
80. clouds
81. poems
82. dumplings
83. miscellaneous
84. summer
85. other seasons
86. the *Spiegel*
87. truth
88. crime novels
89. the weather
90. telephone
91. knife
92. paper
93. plays
94. parents

95. weeds
96. apartments
97. wine
98. cigarettes
99. men
100. women

**On Reading and Writing Liesl Ujvary's Early Work:
Notes from the Translators**

THINGS HAVE CHANGED. Nothing has changed. Both statements are true. The contradictory reality they delineate is inhabited by successive generations of feminists and writers, queer people and queer haters, lovers of law and order, anarchists, and anarchist lovers of law and order. Perhaps the last would be a good description of Liesl Ujvary. Her love of order is another face of her sensitivity to its oppressive, violent, and perverse manifestations. Postwar Europe, in hindsight, presents stuffy conservatism entwined with utopian modernism, ignorance and cleverness in paradoxical pairings. We see modernist homes designed for rituals of an everyday life that seem quaint today, the beginnings of avant-garde ski architecture, the labyrinthine, superregional regulations of everything as well as the human chatter that fills these spaces. It is invigorating to read the uncanniness evoked in these cemented mixtures by their contemporary observer, a young woman axing her way out of them.

Concrete poetry had its heyday in the fifties and sixties, when the contrast with nostalgic moods and privatist pathos staked out a space that seemed yet to fill with new forms of living. New norms would appear as a necessary utopia for a leftist feminist, but while stepping out into the rights afforded by universal definitions, she could in the very same moment observe how they were already tinged with aestheticized chauvinism. When "Peter does everything I say," as well as in the novels about novels, Ujvary construes chunks of virtual reality: a bracketing of the common duty of fiction and a slightly eerie impersonation of a classically male protagonist whose wife appears in the margin like a nameless squeaky toy. It is unclear how outdated the satire is in the age of tradwives on TikTok.

Most words can be left standing. The times seem to swirl around them like tides around the ruins of a pier. But some words become static problems. For example, we were at a loss how to translate the word *Düsenklipper*. Jet clippers? The ship build, not some fancy nail trimming device. We settled on jet planes. And yet the expression may more likely evoke the classy hand dryers found in airport restroom facilities, so much time has passed since Heitor Villa-Lobos evoked the feeling of a new cosmopolitan era with *assobio a jato*. The eros of the word *jet* in its connection with the science of aerodynamics and systems theory of flow has faded to the point of no longer being clearly understood. Something similar has happened to *concrete*, which celebrated the building material with which modernist architecture created some of its most spectacular designs, from churches to bus stops to cooling towers, before sinking back into the plush, classist armchairs of consumer architecture. Spectacle has come to be read as escapism as opposed to celebration of the Schuylerian potential of everyday life. The chiastic relation that design—to which conceptual art is very close—maintains between utopian necessities and aesthetic extravagance is reflected in this 1977 work, with its many-faceted plays on scales of example and generality, norm and exception, pattern and truth. Designing new worlds also happens in language learning, a fundamental and productive experience of alienation in the face of basic sentence structures. In both cases, a repetition of seemingly simple facts triggers their startled and startling revision.

Good & Safe includes numerous examples of serial texts, lists, litanies, repetition and ritual, swiftly installed and swiftly taken back down again as if the author were an illegal street vendor. Logical permutations thrash through the systematic, sounding out its absurdity. These may be early examples of a phenomenon that has exploded in the digital age, ending with the hopeful field of source code philology: text not written to be read by humans. Or: to be read aloud? We found ourselves numbering the lines and reading them out to each other, closing our eyes, groping for the precise gist of the idiom. "How are you?" saunters down through familiar conditions—articulated with a very limited vocabulary by varying word orders—like a river broadening into a delta of glee and misery. The reading experience in such cases veers off the track of linear mimesis, where following line after line is assumed to construct meaning, images, chronological narration in a reading mind. Here the user experience begins in the mind and sometimes reaches its full punch long after the book has been closed. The reader remains in the room, right across from the book, in concrete poetry. But rather than swallowing line after line, one finds oneself jumping across paragraphs and pages, looking to "get" the principle, "get" the joke. Then, in a pause from this scramble, a reader may gaze upon the time and space of its execution like one might at a field of screaming crickets from the safety of a path—in this case the margin of the page. The texts, in other words, raise questions about how to use a poem.

Liesl is no performative reader like Ernst Jandl. The strength is the text, no need for additional theatrical embellishment. People who feel it necessary to raise their voice or entertain with performative antics while reading get on Liesl's nerves. That is, in Austrian literature. She is a fan of Detroit techno and appreciates noise music. In her own music, she sometimes splashes around in wild sawtooth gambols, but soon hones in on sine-tone based regularities, human voice coming through and invariably sensed as gentle, playful, lively, worthy of cherishing. But what is it supposed to say?

In one of the most violent series, a sequence in the part titled "I," dreams, wishes, vows seem to surge out in iambic quatrains. "Someday I'd like to be rosy / someday I'd like to laugh..." Each of these poems is struck out with simple, slightly curved lines, and followed up by poems consisting of statements. "I'm dying because everyone dies. I'm dying because I'm old. I'm dying because there is a war." The poem in question is a good example of the varied powers of over-affirmation employed by Ujvary throughout the book. By listing six reasons one after another, each one of them becomes questionable—we know this from our friends' excuses.

In her later works, Ujvary developed a technique of building text out of lines taken from thrillers, sci-fi, and news reports—here she sometimes seems to be exploring her toolbox, each poem sampling a possible logic of affairs.

From years of friendship with the author, who has been a generous mentor and guide to me, stylistically (always write so that it sounds like a translation) and in matters of life wisdom (take out the trash frequently in summer, it gets smelly), there are several biographical clues that I can provide, but no answers to the big questions—What's she doing? What is poetry? Why? These questions remain for the reader to ponder. Concerning types of wurst, for which I did a Google image search, she coyly remarked: You know more than I do. I know that she taught Russian in Tokyo—at Sophia, the Jesuit university. In Moscow, while enrolled in an advanced study program for Russian teachers, Ujvary was repeatedly invited to conversations with the KGB in empty hotel rooms. She resisted their pressure and returned to Austria without becoming an informant, but as Herta Müller has vividly described, techniques of intimidation have the power to transform someone's reality like a magic wand: a form of malign signification. A wrinkle in the bed, smoothed with a hand, may take on the meaning of a life extinguished. By displacing objects in a victim's house, secret service agents would let their quarry know their private space had been invaded and could be invaded again at any time—this deployment of grounded paranoia is reported by Frank Wilderson III as well as by Müller. In such a context, statements of simple or tautological facts become a way of communicating threats.

Ujvary employs similar techniques to undermine the pretense of innocence in her conservative, post-Nazi society. Shown in technical purity, stripped of its unilateral power, it becomes a potential tool of resistance. The technique is one Ujvary shares with some of the authors of the anthology she smuggled out of Russia, translated, and published in Switzerland a few years before writing *Sicher & Gut*. That anthology, titled *Freiheit ist Freiheit* (*Freedom Is Freedom*) featured poems by Vagrich Bakhchanyan, Igor Kholin, Eduard Limonov, Vladislav Lyon, Vsevolod Nekrasov, and Genrikh Sapgir.

The title of the anthology functions in just that way of polysemy-under-pressure, but this political side of concrete poetry—from the oppressed side, as it were—was unpopular. It resonated, however, with other black humorists such as Ernst Jandl and Helmut Heissenbüttel, allies with whom Liesl Ujvary collaborated, but whose poetry, as translator Erhan Altan recently put it, did not strictly fit the rule set up by the purists that concrete poetry should deal with language as material only, aloof from any form of political or vernacular content. Her working-class sarcasm must have appeared as a provocation to the gatekeepers of concrete poetry at the time, such as Ernst Gomringer and Gerhard Rühm, with their gleeful chauvinism, celebration of billboard aesthetics, and modernism for the moneyed art world. Tautology in the context of unfree speech brings forth an artesian fountain of connotation. A simple expression may start to wander like a questioning and threatening searchlight through the world of the reader. The authors of *Freiheit ist Freiheit* were in jail at the time of its publication. The author of *Good & Safe* is still at large—bad, canny, and dangerous.

Ann Cotten, Tokyo, October 31, 2024

I WAS DRAWN to *Sicher & Gut* by its at once delightful and unnerving juxtapositions, achieved through such apparently simple language. In its focus on the mundane (or concrete) both in subject—the detailed lists of objects laid out on the kitchen table, the repetitive filling of the toilet bowl, the exhaustive enumeration of foods and fluids—and in form ("I want to write a poem in which every line is different"), these texts sometimes feel like daring schoolgirl pranks, sometimes like strange, even transgressive jokes— jokes whose intention is not always clear at first glance, or indeed after many readings. Instead, the meaning of many of these texts creeps in indirectly, by association or precisely because no point seems to be made—in the gathering horror and humor of cigarettes touching mouths in a long chain of objects whose interconnectedness we prefer to ignore, in the accumulating doubt building across ever-more-ambiguous variations of "fine thanks," in the rising tension of gendered household activities carried out as dustclouds swell silently in the distance.

Many of the texts in this book do not immediately look or sound like poems. Liesl Ujvary is an experimental visual and sound artist as well as a writer (her photo series *Hard & soft* presented portraits of colleagues and contemporaries, including Ernst Jandl, Friederike Mayröcker, Bodo Hell, and Elfriede Jelinek, alongside those of psychoactive plants), and her writing too plays visually with form and category. This book's relationship to sound is less obvious. It certainly plays with the registers of childlike, casual, and bureaucratic language, building up and breaking expectations and patterns. The subtle rhythm that builds in these texts through expectation and its disappointment has sometimes been a decisive factor in my understanding, and thus my translation, of them. Many of the poems form lists, often apparently unconnected or nonsensical, yet the rhythm and tension that builds across these texts is unmistakable—in "Do you not sense anything?" or "Instants," for example, but also in the poems where every line repeats. This is why the texts in this collection, though conceptual rather than rhetorical, lend themselves surprisingly well to being read aloud. The reading eye can skim over the repetitive lines of "Peter Stuyvesant" or "I want to write a poem in which every line is different," registering their sameness in an instant and moving on to the next page ("I want to write a poem that does not exist yet"). Only the concept lingers. In contrast, when one hears the text read aloud, the expectation of a turn is newly established with each repetition of the line, and a tension is created that builds to confusion, to disappointment, to foreboding, to humor, and finally to a questioning of the intent, of what is *behind* or *beneath* the words. It is this brilliant building of tension through sound, through the rhythm of uncomfortable repetition, the too-long-drawn-out, that finally forces the reader to question everything about their encounter with the text.

This prying-under the language—the social fabric—of the everyday is to me the most striking and unsettling aspect of this work. Concrete poetry, as Ann once defined it, uses language as both the object and the method of its interrogation. And interrogation seems to be at the core of these texts, whose "suspiciously precise" details (in the words of Ariel Francisco) create a sense that something undefined and monstrous lurks beneath the words and structures of the everyday. We never quite come face to face with the horrors that fester beneath left and right, wine and cognac, shit and skin, men and women, Austrians and foreigners, ovens and long-distance walls. They remain with us, alongside or underneath the surface of traffic rules and sausage skins.

Anna-Isabella Dinwoodie, Berlin, October 2024

thanks

to the Deutscher Übersetzerfonds for their support

to the editors of *Asymptote* and *Fieldnotes* for publishing earlier versions of some of these translations

for translation advice, support, attention to the text, encouraging words, etc.:

yaccaira salvatierra	kim golding
will morningstar	katie machen
vani natarajan	katie long
tom dinwoodie	kareem james abu-zeid
steve bellin-oka	jp allen
sarah audsley	joe gross
roger sedarat	jay alexander brown
rebecca suzuki	jason lamb
ralph klever	jane stringham
petra coronato	jan tabaczynski
paula carter	james loop
paige vega	hillary gulley
noreen cargill	hiatt werling
norbert math	henry gifford
nora carr	gerardo pacheco matus
nicole cooley	francesca hyatt
nichole gleisner	dominik hruza
morgan davis	diana meservey
mónica de la torre	danielle harms
michelle whittaker	corinna anderson
michael bazzett	chandanie somwaru
matvei yankelevich	brigitta falkner
marine cornuet	ariel courage
lupita eyde-tucker	ariel francisco
liesl ujvary	anne posten
kristen herbert	andy su
klein voorhees	amanda hawkins
kiyo kamisawa	abby wender

Liesl Ujvary (b. 1939) is an Austrian writer in the concrete tradition. Her oeuvre includes experimental electronic music and video. In the mid-1970s, after studying Slavic languages, ancient Hebrew literature, and art history in Vienna and Zurich, she edited and translated an anthology of six Soviet poets whose manuscripts she smuggled out of Moscow. Her poetic debut, *Good & Safe* (*Sicher & Gut*), published in 1977 and reissued in 2017, combines conceptual rigor with slapstick and social satire. Later works such as *Body & Tech* (2024) explore existential questions through scenarios of cyborg combat.

Ann Cotten is a writer and translator from Vienna, Austria. Translations from English to German include books by Isabel Waidner, Legacy Russell, Rosmarie Waldrop, Mary MacLane, Joe Wenderoth, and Adam Green. Cotten is co-editor of *Triëdere*, an Austrian journal for theoretical literature.

Anna-Isabella Dinwoodie earned an MFA in translation from Queens College, CUNY, where she served as translations editor at *Armstrong Literary*. She makes visual poetry and performance art. A 2019 Bread Loaf Scholar, Dinwoodie works as a freelance translator and writer in Berlin.

Fatima Naqvi is Leavenworth Professor of German and Film & Media Studies at Yale University. She writes on Austrian authors and filmmakers such as Thomas Bernhard, Elfriede Jelinek, Peter Handke, Friederike Mayröcker, and Michael Haneke.

This book was typeset in Söhne, a contemporary neo-grotesque designed by Kris Sowersby in 2019 for Klim Type Foundry. It is inspired by the "analogue materiality" of Akzidenz-Grotesk, the canonical German sans serif. Cover design by Andrew Bourne based on the original 1977 cover of *Sicher & Gut* published by Rhombus Verlag in Vienna, Austria, and republished by Klever Verlag, Vienna, in 2017. Typesetting by Don't Look Now. Printed and bound in Lithuania by BALTO Print. Manufactured by Arctic Paper in Sweden, the paper in this book meets EU Ecolabel, Forest Stewardship Council, and Cradle to Cradle certification standards.

 WORLD POETRY

Samer Abu Hawwash
Ruins and Other Poems
tr. Huda J. Fakhreddine

Marie-Noëlle Agniau
The Escapades
tr. Jesse Hover Amar

Nadia Anjuman
Smoke Drifts:
Selected Poems
tr. Diana Arterian
& Marina Omar

Jean-Paul Auxeméry
Selected Poems
tr. Nathaniel Tarn

Leire Bilbao
Fish Scales: Selected Poems
tr. Joana Urtasun

Boethius
The Poems from On the
Consolation of Philosophy
tr. Peter Glassgold

Maria Borio
Transparencies
tr. Danielle Pieratti

Astrid Cabral
Spotlight on the Word
tr. Alexis Levitin

Jeannette L. Clariond
Goddesses of Water
tr. Samantha Schnee

Jacques Darras
John Scotus Eriugena
at Laon
tr. Richard Sieburth

Mario dell'Arco
Day Lasts Forever:
Selected Poems
tr. Marc Alan Di Martino

Marie de Quatrebarbes
The Vitals
tr. Aiden Farrell

Ricardo Domeneck
First Epistle to the
Amphibians: Selected Poems
tr. by Chris Daniels

Olivia Elias
Chaos, Crossing
tr. Kareem James Abu-Zeid

Gastón Fernández
Apparent Breviary
tr. KM Cascia

Jerzy Ficowski
Everything I Don't Know
tr. Jennifer Grotz
& Piotr Sommer
PEN AWARD FOR POETRY IN TRANSLATION

Antonio Gamoneda
Book of the Cold
tr. Katherine M. Hedeen &
Víctor Rodríguez Núñez

Mireille Gansel
Soul House
tr. Joan Seliger Sidney

Óscar García Sierra
Houston, I'm the problem
tr. Carmen Yus Quintero

Phoebe Giannisi
Homerica
tr. Brian Sneeden

Zuzanna Ginczanka
On Centaurs & Other Poems
tr. Alex Braslavsky

Julien Gracq
Abounding Freedom
tr. Alice Yang

Karmelo C. Iribarren
You've Heard This One
Before: Selected Poems
tr. John R. Sesgo

Leeladhar Jagoori
What of the Earth
Was Saved
tr. Matt Reeck

Nakedness Is My End:
Poems from the Greek
Anthology
tr. Edmund Keeley

Birhan Keskin
Earthly Conditions:
Selected Poems
tr. Öykü Tekten

Jazra Khaleed
The Light That Burns Us
ed. Karen Van Dyck

Judith Kiros
O
tr. Kira Josefsson

Dimitra Kotoula
The Slow Horizon
That Breathes
tr. Maria Nazos

Maria Laina
Hers
tr. Karen Van Dyck

Maria Laina
Rose Fear
tr. Sarah McCann

Perrin Langda
A Few Microseconds on
Earth
tr. Pauline Levy Valensi

Anna Malihon
Girl with a Bullet
tr. Olena Jennings

Afrizal Malna
Document Shredding
Museum
tr. Daniel Owen

Joyce Mansour
In the Glittering Maw:
Selected Poems
tr. C. Francis Fisher

Manuel Maples Arce
Stridentist Poems
tr. KM Cascia

Selma Meerbaum-Eisinger
Blütenlese
tr. Carlie Hoffman

Ennio Moltedo
Night
tr. Marguerite Feitlowitz

Meret Oppenheim
The Loveliest Vowel Empties: Collected Poems
tr. Kathleen Heil

Giovanni Pascoli
Last Dream
tr. Geoffrey Brock
RAIZISS/DE PALCHI TRANSLATION AWARD

Gabriel Pomerand
Saint Ghetto of the Loans
tr. Michael Kasper & Bhamati Viswanathan

Liliana Ponce
Theory of the Voice and Dream
tr. Michael Martin Shea

Rainer Maria Rilke
Where the Paths Do Not Go
tr. Burton Pike

Amelia Rosselli
Document
tr. Roberta Antognini & Deborah Woodard

Elisabeth Rynell
Night Talks
tr. Rika Lesser

Waly Salomão
Border Fare
tr. Maryam Monalisa Gharavi

George Sarantaris
Abyss and Song: Selected Poems
tr. Pria Louka

George Seferis
Book of Exercises II
tr. Jennifer R. Kellogg
ELIZABETH CONSTANTINIDES MEMORIAL TRANSLATION PRIZE

Seo Jung Hak
The Cheapest France in Town
tr. Megan Sungyoon

Ahmad Shamlou
Elegies of the Earth: Selected Poems
tr. Niloufar Talebi

Edith Södergran
Modern Woman
tr. CD Eskilson

Ardengo Soffici
Simultaneities & Lyric Chemisms
tr. Olivia E. Sears

Liesl Ujvary
Good & Safe
tr. Ann Cotten & Anna-Isabella Dinwoodie

Paul Verlaine
Before Wisdom: The Early Poems
tr. Keith Waldrop & K.A. Hays

Haris Vlavianos
Renaissance
tr. Patricia Barbeito

Witold Wirpsza
Apotheosis of Music
tr. Frank L. Vigoda

Uljana Wolf
kochanie, today i bought bread
tr. Greg Nissan

Ye Lijun
My Mountain Country
tr. Fiona Sze-Lorrain

Verónica Zondek
Cold Fire
tr. Katherine Silver